HCI Theory

Classical, Modern, and Contemporary

Synthesis Lectures on Human-Centered Informatics

Editor
John M. Carroll, *Penn State University*

Human-Centered Informatics (HCI) is the intersection of the cultural, the social, the cognitive, and the aesthetic with computing and information technology. It encompasses a huge range of issues, theories, technologies, designs, tools, environments and human experiences in knowledge work, recreation and leisure activity, teaching and learning, and the potpourri of everyday life. The series will publish state-of-the-art syntheses, case studies, and tutorials in key areas. It will share the focus of leading international conferences in HCI.

HCI Theory: Classical, Modern, and Contemporary
Yvonne Rogers
2012

Activity Theory in HCI: Fundamentals and Reflections
Victor Kaptelinin and Bonnie Nardi
2012

Conceptual Models: Core to Good Design
Jeff Johnson and Austin Henderson
2011

Geographical Design: Spatial Cognition and Geographical Information Science
Stephen C. Hirtle
2011

User-Centered Agile Methods
Hugh Beyer
2010

Experience-Centered Design: Designers, Users, and Communities in Dialogue
Peter Wright and John McCarthy
2010

HCI Theory: Classical, Modern, and Contemporary

Yvonne Rogers

www.morganclaypool.com

ISBN: 9781608459001   paperback
ISBN: 9781608459018   ebook

DOI 10.2200/S00418ED1V01Y201205HCI014

A Publication in the Morgan & Claypool Publishers series
SYNTHESIS LECTURES ON HUMAN-CENTERED INFORMATICS

Lecture #14
Series Editor: John M. Carroll, *Penn State University*
Series ISSN
Synthesis Lectures on Human-Centered Informatics
Print 1946-7680   Electronic 1946-7699

HCI Theory

Classical, Modern, and Contemporary

Yvonne Rogers

UCLIC, University College London, UK

SYNTHESIS LECTURES ON HUMAN-CENTERED INFORMATICS #14

MORGAN & CLAYPOOL PUBLISHERS

ABSTRACT

Theory is the bedrock of many sciences, providing a rigorous method to advance knowledge, through testing and falsifying hypotheses about observable phenomena. To begin with, the nascent field of HCI followed the scientific method borrowing theories from cognitive science to test theories about user performance at the interface. But HCI has emerged as an eclectic interdiscipline rather than a well-defined science. It now covers all aspects of human life, from birth to bereavement, through all manner of computing, from device ecologies to nano-technology. It comes as no surprise that the role of theory in HCI has also greatly expanded from the early days of scientific testing to include other functions such as describing, explaining, critiquing, and as the basis for generating new designs. The book charts the theoretical developments in HCI, both past and present, reflecting on how they have shaped the field. It explores both the rhetoric and the reality: how theories have been conceptualized, what was promised, how they have been used and which has made the most impact in the field — and the reasons for this. Finally, it looks to the future and asks whether theory will continue to have a role, and, if so, what this might be.

KEYWORDS

HCI theory, frameworks, models, design implications, third-wave HCI

In memory of Mike

Contents

Preface

Human-computer interaction (HCI) has grown enormously in its relatively short history since becoming a field in its own right in the early 1980s. As per Shneiderman (2011, p10), *"we've grown from a small rebellious group of researchers who struggled to gain recognition as they broke disciplinary boundaries to a broad influential community with potent impact on the daily lives of every human."* In an attempt to keep up with unprecedented technological developments, HCI has emerged as an eclectic interdiscipline rather than a well-defined science. While it was concerned at its inception primarily with the interface between a user and a computer it now covers all aspect of human life, from birth to bereavement, through all manner of computing, from device ecologies to nano-technology.

One reason for HCI's remarkable expansion is its unremitting desire to address whatever seems fit; from critiquing domestic life to building brain-computer interfaces. No longer only about designing computers that are easy to use, learn and remember, it considers itself capable of commenting and capitalizing on technologies in far-reaching ways, from helping save the planet to encouraging world peace. Several HCI researchers have begun to reflect on the enormity of the burgeoning field: from what is studied, designed and evaluated. Likewise, I consider it timely to take stock and think both about our achievements and our future. Whereas Grudin (2012) thoughtfully charted HCI's checkered history, populated by the people who made it, the landmark research that stands out and the legacy technologies and interfaces that changed our lives, the focus of this book is the theoretical developments in HCI, both past and present, examining how they have shaped the field. In particular, I explore both the rhetoric and the reality: how theories have been conceptualized, what was promised, how they have been used and which has made the most impact in the field — and the reasons for this. I also look to the future and ask whether theory will continue to play a prominent role in research and, if so, what this might be, given the ever-changing challenges we face.

Ten years ago the "user experience" (UX) was all the rage. There was much excitement about what it meant in terms of engagement, enjoyment, fun and even the "felt" experience (Rogers et al., 2011). The UX rapidly became popularized in practice, replacing the "user-friendly" slogan of old school HCI. It was the essence of what people came into contact with, and referred to any artifact, including "newspapers, ketchup bottles, reclining armchairs, cardigans, sweaters" (Garrett, 2010, p10). This widening of HCI has given researchers the license to explore and reflect upon every nook and cranny of life, and to experiment with all manner of technologies, conjuring up and writing about topics that would have been inconceivable just a few years before, such as digitally enabled sex toys (Bardzell and Bardzell, 2011).

Many others from all walks of academic life started to join the field, taking turns dismissing and rejecting the early vanguards of HCI, and suggesting alternative ways of conceptualizing users, interactions and the user experience. Some argued for ousting old school HCI (N.B. The field is only about 30 years old) in favor of different paradigms, such as the third wave (Harrison et al., 2011, 2007). In the 2000s, interaction design became the new HCI (Löwgren and Stolterman, 2004; Preece et al., 2003).

But what do such rapid and radical changes mean for a nascent field, such as HCI? The paint has barely dried for one theory before a new coat is applied. It makes it difficult for anything to become established and widely used. Judging by the diversity of papers that are now accepted at the annual flagship U.S. conference, CHI, and its galaxy of sister venues (e.g., ItalCHI, NordCHI, SouthCHI, OzCHI), there is no longer a coherent set of aims or goals, or accepted classification of contributing disciplines. It seems anything goes and anyone can join in. The early mantra of HCI "know your user" has in a few years all but been superseded by the socially aware slogan "make an impact." Instead of striving to fix interfaces so they are easy and obvious how to use, the community is looking at how it can transform the world to be a better place.

Such flux would seem alien to established disciplines, such as physics and chemistry. Breaking the mold requires a paradigm shift with a good deal of momentum. Within HCI, however, deep roots have not had time to take a hold and so it is easier to go with the flow. The field is a follower. Today, it is very much in tune with contemporary societal concerns. Its motivation has shifted from efficiency and profit towards altruism and alleviating fear — there is a strong desire and belief that we can help improve the lives of those who are impoverished or disadvantaged through designing innovative technology solutions.

Given these new expectations, how does a researcher, designer or student of HCI know where to begin to look for inspiration? The purpose of this book is to help them on their journey by charting and critiquing the various theoretical developments throughout the history of HCI. It examines the utility of the conceptual tools and analytic methods that have been imported, adapted and developed, and how they have grounded concerns, problems and new opportunities through their theoretical framing. Specifically, it asks how applicable they are in terms of how can they help researchers and designers scope, manage and make sense of the space they choose to look at, work in or analyze.

A central theme is how and why HCI theory keeps changing its spots. Part of the reason is a perceived need to continuously invent new theories in order to keep up with the changes afoot that beset HCI practice. A recurring question this raises is the extent to which new insights and applicable tools can be delivered that others, besides those producing them, can and will use. The book discusses what this medley of theories might be and ends by speculating how new approaches are faring against the changing world of research, design and practice.

Yvonne Rogers
May 2012

Acknowledgments

Many thanks to Liam Bannon, Ann Blandford, Jack Carroll, Gilbert Cockton, Dominic Furniss, Beki Grinter, Jonathan Grudin, Eva Hornecker, Ben Shneiderman and Erik Stolterman for providing extensive and thoughtful comments on earlier drafts of the book. I would also like to thank Gary and Gil Marsden for their fantastic hospitality and to acknowledge the EPSRC for giving me time during my dream fellowship to complete this project.

Yvonne Rogers
May 2012

Figure Credits

Figure 1.1   Rogers, Y., Preece, J. & Sharp, H. 2011. *Interaction Design: Beyond Human-Computer Interaction.* 3rd edition. Blackwell Publishing. Copyright ©2011, Wiley. Used with permission.

Figure 4.1   Rogers, Y., Preece, J. & Sharp, H. 2011. *Interaction Design: Beyond Human-Computer Interaction.* 3rd edition. Blackwell Publishing. Copyright ©2011, Wiley. Used with permission.

Figure 4.2   Olson, J.S. and Olson, G.M. 1991. The growth of cognitive modeling in human-computer interaction since GOMS. *Human Computer Interaction,* 5, 221-265. Copyright ©1991, Taylor and Francis. Used with permission.

Figure 6.1   Harper, R., Rodden, T., Rogers, Y. & Sellen, A. 2008. *Being Human: HCI in the Year 2020.* Copyright ©2008, Microsoft. Used with permission from Microsoft.

CHAPTER 1

Introduction

The world is messy, fuzzy, sticky,
theoretically 'tis all quite tricky. (Tom Erickson, 2002)

1.1   BURGEONING HCI

The field of human-computer interaction has burst its seams. Its mission, raison d'être, goals and methodologies, that were established early on, have expanded and dissolved to the point that "HCI is now effectively a boundless domain" (Barnard et al., 2000, p221). Everything is in flux, arguably, more so than ever before: the theory that drives research is changing, a flurry of new concepts have emerged, the domains, topics and user experiences being studied have diversified; many of the ways of doing design are new and much of the technology and user experience that is being designed for, in terms of platforms, applications, services, ecologies, etc., is significantly different from ten years ago. The focus is no longer about human-computer interaction *per se*, but more about "the creation of intuitive, simple, transparent interaction designs which allow people to easily express themselves through various computationally enhanced tools and media." (Bannon, 2011a, p17). These changes reflect and capitalize on the rapid advances that have occurred in computing and computation (see Grudin, 2012, for an extensive historical overview of HCI and related fields).

While potentially much is to be gained from such burgeoning growth, the downside is a worrying lack of direction, structure and purpose in the field. What was originally a confined problem space with a clear focus that adopted a small set of methods to tackle it — that of designing computer systems to make them more easy and efficient to use by a single user — has now turned into a more diffuse space with a less clear purpose as to what to study, what to design for and which methods to use. It is now widely accepted that a specific problem space does not have to be identified, but an opportunity to design for the unimagined and possible, is suffice. Moreover, global challenges that previously were considered the realms of government and politics are now being promoted as major research topics for HCI, for example, reducing global poverty through social media, mobile and other technologies (see Shneiderman, 2011). At the same time, some have moved into uncharted territories where even taboo subjects are analyzed. Many more topics, areas and approaches are being published in HCI venues, including technology-enhanced sex, religion and food.

It is inevitable for a field that has become increasingly concerned with society, everyday living and progress to have growing pains. A danger, however, of a nascent field, growing so fast and without checks, is it spiraling out of control. There is no longer a consensus of its purpose or indeed what criteria to use to assess its contribution and value to knowledge and practice. No sooner does an official body, such as the ACM, derive a charter for HCI, it is out of date. For example, the definition of HCI prescribed by ACM's SIGCHI on its website (SIGCHI, 2012) is restricted to "the study and practice of the design, implementation, use, and evaluation of interactive computing systems," whereas there is much more happening in HCI today — judging by what is presented at conferences, workshops, etc., and discussed in the blogosphere. Do we try to stem the tide and impose some order and rules or let the field continue to expand in an unruly fashion?

[handwritten margin note: As if "we" have some say in the matter ?!]

Is HCI now CSCW, Human Factors and Ubicomp, too?

Human-computer interaction (HCI) is generally accepted as the umbrella term for a field that includes and overlaps with several other fields and areas (see Figure 1.1).

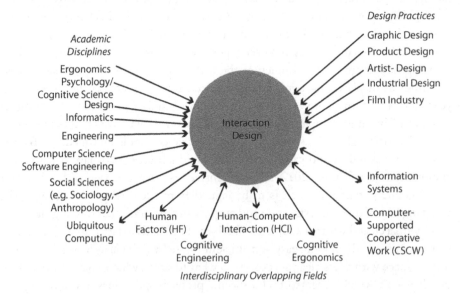

Figure 1.1: The relationship between contributing academic disciplines, design practices and interdisciplinary fields concerned with interaction design (from Rogers et al., 2011).

The initial vision was of an applied science that could use cognitive science theories and methods to inform the development of software (see Carroll, 2003). The goal was to understand how people make use of computational systems and devices and how they could be designed to be usable and useful. Since its inception, several other fields and approaches concerned with people, design and technology have emerged, some splintering from HCI and others evolving from different disciplines; these include CSCW, Ubicomp, cognitive ergonomics, social computing and interaction design. The difference between these and HCI is largely one of focus, in terms of the different methods, philosophies and lenses that are used to study, analyze, and design computers. Another is the scope and problems they address, where specific kinds of topics may be emphasized. For example, Information Systems is concerned with the application of computing technology in domains like business, health and education, whereas Computer-Supported Cooperative Work (CSCW) broke away from HCI's single user unit of analysis, at the time, to focus on how to support multiple people working together using computer systems (Greif, 1988).

While the newer fields have carved out their distinctiveness in terms of framing, rhetoric and identity to set them apart from each other and HCI, HCI keeps recasting its net ever wider, which has the effect of subsuming them. For example, the topics covered by many papers that first appeared in a CSCW or an Ubicomp conference are now equally at home in the ACM's CHI conference. While it is in the interest of the "other" fields to maintain their distinct boundaries and separateness from HCI, HCI does not have to reciprocate. Its tendency towards inclusiveness means it will continue to expand, sometimes at the expense of others losing ground.

In an attempt to pin down a definition that reflected the changes a foot in the field, Jenny Preece, Helen Sharp and myself chose the title *Interaction Design: Beyond HCI* for the three editions of our textbook (Preece et al., 2003; Rogers et al., 2011; Sharp et al., 2007). We considered the term Human-Computer Interaction was no longer representative, with its focus on a single user and computer. Instead, the more general term "interaction design" was considered to be more encompassing, covering a wider range of design, people (sic) and interaction aspects: "designing interactive products to support the way people communicate and interact in their everyday and working lives." (Rogers et al., 2011, p9) But even this definition misses out on much of the day-to-day practice of interaction design, both in academe and industry. In particular, it fails to capture recent trends, for example, of putting human values first, such as ethics (Harper et al., 2008) and moves towards doing research "in-the-wild" (Rogers, 2011).

Are there non-human values?

1.2   CONCEPTUALIZING HCI: FROM PARADIGMS TO FRAMEWORKS

A number of sources of inspiration and knowledge have been used to inform design and guide research in HCI, including paradigms, theories, models, frameworks and approaches (Carroll, 2003; Rogers et al., 2011). These vary in terms of their scale and specificity to a particular problem space. At the highest level is a *paradigm;* this refers to a general approach that has been adopted by a community of researchers and designers for carrying out their work, in terms of shared assumptions, concepts, values and practices. At the next level is a *theoretical approach* or *perspective* that refers more generally to the assumptions about a phenomenon being studied or designed for, the lenses used to analyze it and the questions asked, that are grounded in a theoretical tradition, for example, within social psychology, design or engineering. A *theory* is a well-substantiated explanation of some aspect of a phenomenon, for example, the theory of information processing that explains how the mind, or some aspect of it, is assumed to work. A *model* is a simplification of some aspect of HCI, intended to make it easier for designers to predict and evaluate alternative designs. A *framework* is a set of interrelated concepts and/or a set of specific questions that is intended to inform a particular domain area, e.g., collaborative learning, online communities or an analytic method, e.g., ethnographic studies. A number of frameworks have been introduced in HCI to help designers constrain and scope the user experience for which they are designing. They can come in a variety of forms, including steps, questions, concepts, challenges, principles, tactics and dimensions. For example, there are frameworks for helping designers think about how to conceptualize learning, working, socializing, fun, emotion, etc. and others that focus on how to design particular kinds of technologies to evoke certain responses, e.g., persuasive technologies and pleasurable products.

HCI Paradigms

In general, a paradigm provides a set of practices that a community has agreed upon (Rogers et al., 2011). These include:

- questions to be asked and how they should be framed;
- phenomena to be observed;
- how findings from studies are to be analyzed and interpreted.

In the late 1970s and 1980s, the prevailing paradigm in human-computer interaction was how to design user-centered applications for the desktop computer. Carroll (2003) talks about this first decade of HCI as the Golden Age — in the sense that there was a general agreement about what it was about, what it strove for and what it could achieve — which it turns out was considerable. Questions about what and how to design were framed in terms of specifying the requirements for a single user interacting with a screen-based interface. Task analytic and usability methods were developed based on an individual user's cognitive capabilities. The acronym WIMP was used as a way of characterizing the core features of an interface for a single user: this stood for Windows, Icons, Menus and Pointer. This was later superseded by the GUI (graphical user interface), a term that has stuck with us ever since. Within interaction design, many changes took place in the mid-to-late 1990s. The WIMP interface with its single thread, discrete event dialog was considered to be unnecessarily limiting (e.g., Jacob, 1996). Instead, many argued that a new paradigm was needed to enable more flexible forms of interaction to take place, having a higher degree of interactivity and parallel input/output exchanges. A shift in thinking, together with several technological advances, paved the way for a new way of conceptualizing human-computer interaction. The rhetoric "beyond the desktop" became a pervasive starting point, resulting in many new challenges, questions and phenomena being considered. New methods of designing, modeling, and analyzing came to the fore. At the same time, new theories, concepts and ideas entered the stage. Weiser's (1991) vision of the future also provided an alternative paradigm in the field of ubiquitous computing.

To summarize, paradigms, theories, models and frameworks are not mutually exclusive but overlap in their way of conceptualizing the problem and design space, varying in their level of rigor, abstraction and purpose. Paradigms are overarching approaches that comprise a set of accepted practices and framing of questions and phenomena to observe; theories tend to be comprehensive, explaining human-computer interactions; models tend to simplify some aspect of human-computer interaction, providing a basis for designing and evaluating systems; and frameworks provide a set of core concepts, questions or principles to consider when designing for a user experience. Within HCI, many researchers attempted to develop different kinds of conceptual tools that could be applied to HCI and interaction design.

But as the new approaches, ideas and theories proliferate within HCI, it can make it problematic for those inside and outside to know what are the current acceptable, reliable, useful and generalizable findings and advances in knowledge. Researchers and designers, alike, also find it more difficult to say with confidence what HCI is, and to know which of the many tools and techniques to use, when doing design and research. The criteria available for them to help make systematic judgments are often disparate, and many a student may select a technique, theory and set of methods on a "pick and mix" basis. Some might argue that such arbitrariness does not matter so long as the outcomes of HCI can be shown to have an impact on society that is supported by evidence. Others, however, feel uncomfortable that the field is losing its rigor and reason.

Nearly ten years ago I addressed these concerns in an extensive review paper about the impact of the then recent developments of theory in HCI practice, by taking stock and reflecting on the numerous changes that were happening (Rogers, 2004). I critiqued the seminal theoretical developments of the time, assessing and ruminating more generally on the role of theory in HCI. A core concern running through the review article was the extent to which theory was used in design practice. I noted how a diversity of new theories had been imported and adapted in the field. A key question I raised was whether these attempts had been productive in terms of knowledge transfer. By knowledge transfer, I was referring to the translation of research findings (e.g., theory, empirical results, descriptive accounts, cognitive models) from one discipline (e.g., cognitive psychology, sociology) into practical concerns that could be applied to another (e.g., HCI, CSCW). An empirical study of designer's use of theory that I conducted made for rather depressing reading, especially for those championing theory in practice (Rogers, 2004). Despite designers' perceived need and desire for applying theory, they reported in the survey that they were only able to make use of some of it in a limited way. I concluded by proposing new knowledge transfer mechanisms, including a lingua franca that designers and researchers, alike, could use to talk to one another more.

1.3 AIMS OF THE BOOK

So what next? The purpose of this book is, firstly, to revisit the concerns surrounding the role of theory in an applied and rapidly changing field, by examining its place and value in the field in the interim years. Secondly, to consider the ramifications of this for a field that has become everything and anything, in an attempt to keep up with, understand and be part of a technology-pervasive world that is radically transforming how we live. Thirdly, to discuss what it means for the advancement of a field and its knowledge where its theory industry has become so multifarious.

Clearly, it is impossible to do justice to all the theories that have been imported and written about in HCI (and overlapping disciplines) in one book. There is inevitable bias in what is covered here; some theories are covered in depth, while some are briefly touched upon (such as those in CSCW and cognitive ergonomics). My objective here is to provide an overview of the theoretical developments, but to give more space to those that have been most influential in HCI (e.g., Distributed Cognition, Activity Theory), providing more in-depth discussion of their use and impact. For each theory, I describe how it has been imported, adapted and its impact on research and practice. I have also included a number of approaches that are not considered to be theoretical but are *methodological* in nature. The reason for their inclusion is that they have played an integral part in other theoretical developments within HCI. These are primarily grounded theory and ethnography and I have also included *approaches* that are considered largely or wholly *atheoretical,* namely, ethnomethodology and situated action. These were included because of their impact. Besides being influential in shaping the field, they have often been highly critical of existing theories in HCI, and alternatively, promoting radically different ways of framing human-computer interactions, phenomena and data.

As Grudin notes (personal communication), a *method,* such as an experiment or observation, is not a theory. However, the outcome of using a method to collect data is often used as input for theory construction or theory testing and hence, in my view, it is important to consider methods in relation to theory. While it is generally accepted that there is a distinction between method and theory, it is argued that they are intertwined, especially in terms of how they are used and developed in HCI. Hence, my position in this book is to adopt a broad-brush approach to theory in HCI. Instead of restricting myself to using the term "theory" in the narrow scientific tradition, I have chosen to show how theory, in all its forms and guises, has been adapted and contextualized in HCI practice.

1.4   PARALLELS WITH ART HISTORY

To frame the history of HCI theory, I borrow, loosely, from the periodization of the History of Art, characterizing it in terms of three parallel movements: Classical, Modern and Contemporary. I critique *Classical* theoretical developments and the role they have played in the field, followed by an overview of *Modern* and *Contemporary* theories. Previous attempts to characterize the history and the significant developments in HCI have conceptualized them more generally in metaphorical terms of waves, paradigms or circles (e.g., Bødker, 2006; Grudin, 1990; Harrison et al., 2007). My intention of adding yet another framing to the mix — this time as parallels to epochs in the History of Art — is to provide a different historical lens, which, I think, lends itself to understanding the way different theories have come and gone, and the zeitgeist behind their development. The parallel with the History of Art is at the level of distinctive periods, such as Classicism and Modernism that denote the style and philosophy of the art or theory produced during each of them.

Classical Art began with the Greeks and Romans and their interpretation and formal representation of the human form and the environment in which it exists. It adheres to artistic principles and rules laid down by painters and sculptors. Much training was required to become an artist of classicism. Well-known movements included Gothic, Baroque, Flemish and Pre-Raphaelite. Modern art took over in the late 19th century and lasted until the 1970s. This period is associated with art in which the previous classical traditions were thrown aside in the spirit of new ideas and experimentation, rethinking the nature of materials and the function of art. Notably, there was a move towards *abstraction*. For instance, Henri Matisse, Georges Braque, André Derain and Raoul Dufy totally transformed the Parisian art world with wild, expressive landscapes and figure paintings. Contemporary art then emerged in the 1960s/70s and is still with us today as the dominant movement. There are many different kinds of contemporary art, including well-known ones such as pop art, performance art and postmodern art and more obscure ones such as VJ art, cynical realism and superstroke. Collectively, contemporary art is considered to be more self conscious and socially conscious than previous eras, concerning itself with popular culture and political developments of the time, including feminism, multiculturalism and conceptualism.

Similar to these three periods of art history, the defining spirit or mood of the three eras of HCI theory can be viewed as being underpinned by the ideas and beliefs of the time. The Classical HCI period imported cognitive theory in a rigorous and constrained way; the Modernist HCI period saw a broader and colorful palette of approaches and uses of theory — from social, phenomenological and cognitive science — while the Contemporary period became more value-led, drawing from a range of moralistic and societal-based perspectives. Each has significantly extended the discourse of HCI research.

However, at the same time, many of the theoretically based approaches that have been promulgated in each period have had only a limited impact on the *practice* of interaction design. Why is this so? The book discusses this dilemma and concludes that HCI theory is now at a crossroads. It can continue to address moderately sized issues (i.e., small HCI) or it can try to tackle even bigger challenges (i.e., big HCI). While modernist theories can continue to deal with micro HCI, having an input into the design of new experiences and technologies, different kinds of theories are needed to better articulate and ground macro-HCI, to encompass the complex challenges facing society (Shneiderman, 2012).

In the next chapter, I provide a brief overview of how HCI grew alongside the technological developments that were taking place. In Chapter 3, I summarize the various roles and contributions theory has made to HCI. Then in Chapters 4, 5 and 6, I provide an overview of the three periods of HCI theory. Chapter 7 discusses the reasons behind the success and failures of theory being applied in practice. Finally, Chapter 8 looks to the future, asking where theory will go next.

CHAPTER 2

The Backdrop to HCI Theory

"There is nothing so practical as a good theory." (Kurt Levin, 1951)

2.1   TRANSFORMING SOCIETY

The arrival and rapid pace of technological developments in the last few years (e.g., the internet, wireless technologies, mobile phones, pervasive technologies, GPS, multi-touch displays) has led to an escalation of new opportunities for augmenting, extending and supporting a range of user experiences, interactions and communications. These include designing experiences for all manner of people (and not just *users*) in all manner of settings doing all manner of things. The home, the crèche, the outdoors, public places and even the human body are now being experimented with as potential places to embed computational devices. A wide-reaching range of human activities is now being analyzed and an equally eye-popping set of innovative technologies proposed to support them, to the extent of invading previously private aspects of our lives (e.g., domestic life and personal hygiene). A consequence is that "the interface" is no longer about the WIMP or the GUI, but has become ubiquitous, being viewed as invisible, natural and everywhere. Computer-based interactions can take place through many kinds of surfaces and in many different places. As such, many different ways of interacting with computationally based systems are now possible, ranging from that which we are conscious of controlling (e.g., using a keyboard with a computer monitor) to that which we may be unaware of how we manage it (e.g., our brain waves moving cursors on screens and moving sensor-controlled tangibles).

Simply, the world has become suffused with technologies that have profoundly changed how we live. Computers have intruded in our lives as well as disappeared into the world around us; they now monitor as well as guide us; and worrying for some, they have even begun coercing us to change our behavior. They increasingly have become part of our everyday environment, in public spaces such as airports, garages and shopping malls, as well as in the private spaces of our homes.

Clark (2004) proposed the *extended mind theory*, where our minds have now extended into the world to the point that technology has now become part of us. For example, it is now common place for people to use online calendars to remind themselves to send a birthday card to a friend or Google information on their smart phones during ongoing conversations at dinner parties to name an actor or produce a factoid that may be on the tip of everyone's tongue but unable to be mentally recalled by anyone. On first owning an iPhone or an iPad, people noticed how it started taking over more and more of their brain functions, increasingly replacing and augmenting parts of their memory, such as storing addresses and numbers that once would have required cognitive effort to recall. In-car GPS systems have also replaced map reading skills; many drivers now follow instructions reducing the cognitive effort that was needed to work out the best route. For an increasingly number of them, it is becoming unimaginable not to be aided in this way (Chalmers, 2008). They are no longer cognitive amplifiers or aids; they have become an integral part of us, how we interact with the environment and each other.

At the same time affordable computing devices, especially cell phones, are becoming more accessible across the globe. More people than ever are now using a cell phone or other computing device, be they a retiree in New Zealand, a schoolchild in Africa or a farmer in Outer Mongolia. The way children learn is also changing as more and more technologies are assimilated into their lives. For example, how it happens (e.g., taking part in a discussion with people from all over the world) and when it happens (e.g., listening to a podcast about pollution while cycling home) is changing. The number of elderly people is increasing as a proportion of the total population. Those growing old in the next ten years will have become accustomed to using computers and cell phones in their work and leisure. Hence, the need to design computer applications for old people who have not used email or the internet will no longer be a major concern but designing social network sites, creative tools, etc., for healthy, active 70-, 80-year olds and beyond, will.

Technological developments, therefore, are not only altering the way we grow up and grow old, but pervading almost every aspect of our daily lives, from how we shop to how we look after ourselves, increasing our reliance on them. We are spending more time, and devoting more effort to being in touch with each other than ever before. Our unbridled desire to keep in touch is equaled by our desire to capture more information about our lives and our doings than ever before. What it means to record, why we record and what we do with the collected materials is also changing. This is happening not just at a personal level, but also at the level of government, institutions and agencies.

For the HCI researcher, such developments pose new moral design questions: should they continue to design ever more digital prosthetic aids for people, so they no longer have to think or learn how to accomplish a task by themselves? Or, should a line be drawn, where the designer says no to the seemingly latest preposterous idea, such as a computer agent taking over major policy-making decisions, or at the other end of the spectrum, reminding someone when to go to the toilet or clean their teeth? Is it desirable and socially acceptable to continuously suggest, create and swamp human life with every conceivable technology augmentation? Moreover, how can theories about what it means to be human and technology augmented help the researcher address these concerns?

2.2   HCI'S GROWING PAINS

How are researchers in HCI and those who practice "UX design" keeping up with and responding to the technological changes? Should they continue to do what they know best, applying their armory of methods in order to improve the interfaces for existing products, or should they divert their time to designing and creating new technological products, now that it is easier to make prototypes and much more affordable to do so? It seems the HCI community is increasingly doing both, plying their trade in inventive and evolutionary ways. In order to keep abreast and be valued, HCI research and design has had to change: from what it examines, the lenses it uses and what it had to offer. It no longer confines itself to being about "user-centered design," but has set its sights on pastures new, embracing much broader and far-reaching agendas. Following the dot.com bubble in the mid-late 1990s and the social media revolution in the early 2000s, what the field has attempted to improve, design and facilitate has snowballed. HCI research has changed irrevocably. The list of topics is diverse, from emotional, eco-friendly, and embodied experiences to context, constructivism and culture.

Part of the new order came about as a reaction to what HCI researchers saw happening in the world, especially the ways ubiquitous technologies proliferated and so rapidly transformed how people lived their lives (Bell and Dourish, 2007). Another reason was the many new opportunities offered to HCI researchers to not always be one step behind reworking poorly designed interfaces, but to be ahead of the game, becoming inventors, tinkerers and designers, themselves, creating new apps, services, interventions, prototypes and devices. The technological developments, coupled with many innovative HCI up-to-date curricula, has meant that a new generation of researchers have come to the forefront, with a much wider skill set than previous ones, no longer dependent on others doing the building and the implementing. They are joining forces with the Maker's Movement; where innovative interfaces and user experiences are created and experimented with in-the-wild, opening up new avenues of research.

Much has been gained from this rapid expansion. However, the downside has been growing pains, in terms of not being able to establish a clearly defined identity (Grudin, 2006). It became much more difficult to explain, justify or account for the funding, the findings and the acceptability of the research. The trivial and the serious began to sit side-by-side where anything became potentially a topic for HCI (Rogers, 2009). When asked what we do for a living, many of us began to find it increasingly difficult to explain in a sentence, in the way HCI researchers used to do 10 years ago, e.g., "designing computers to be easy to use." Instead, there is much fumbling with adjectives and fuzzy slogans, such as "designing engaging computer interfaces" and "what it means to be human in a world full of computers." We often find ourselves talking about specific projects, such as "I am concerned with the privacy issues surrounding how web, mobile and sensor-based technologies track your every move or click" and resort to using everyday examples such as the iPhone by way of illustration.

While "living without parental controls" (Grudin, 2007) can be liberating in a rapidly transforming society, the questions HCI researchers ask, the purpose of their endeavors and the motivation behind them still need scrutiny, debate and reflection, especially if their outputs are to be of relevance and value to society. Part of this entails setting new agendas, determining what to throw out and what new topics and concerns to focus on. Even its very core — prescribing usability (i.e., how to design easy-to-use tools) — needs rethinking given that *using* technology is becoming second nature in its various manifestations to many people. The classic interface horror stories, such as the flashing VCR, have been superseded by more pressing matters that face society in the 21st century, such as how pervasive technologies are intruding and extending our physical bodies, cognitive minds and social lives. What does it mean to have 500+ friends online but not a best friend to hang out with everyday after school and share deep secrets with? What does it mean to know how many calories someone has burned, hours slept or energy consumed but to not know how to cook, sleep properly, or be able to switch a light on or off manually? These are the concerns that the HCI community is beginning to wrestle with, explicating what it means to be human in an age of ubiquitous computing (Harper et al., 2008).

2.3   ADOLESCENT HCI

In an attempt to keep up with and address the new challenges, significant strides have been made in academia and industry, alike, to extend HCI, by developing a wider set of methodologies and practices. Innovative design methods, unheard of in the 1980s, have been imported and adapted from far afield to study and investigate what people did in diverse settings. Ethnography, informant design, cultural probes, technology probes and scenario-based design are examples of these. Alternative ways of conceptualizing the field have also emerged. For example, usability has been re-operationalized, in terms of a range of user experience goals (e.g., aesthetically pleasing, motivating) in addition to the traditional set of efficiency goals. The concept of funology also came to the forefront, where it became widely acceptable to study and design for user experiences that were to do with enjoyment, aesthetics and the experience of use (Blythe et al., 2008; Hassenzahl, 2001).

The desktop paradigm has been largely replaced by a new way of thinking about technology as being everywhere, invisible and embedded in the environment. New phrases were coined to reflect this: ubiquitous computing, pervasive computing and the "Internet of Things." The main thrust behind ubiquitous computing came from the late Mark Weiser (1991), whose vision was for computers to disappear into the environment in a way that we would no longer be aware of them and would use them without thinking about them. Similarly, a main idea behind pervasive computing was that people should be able to access and interact with information any place and any time using a seamless integration of technologies. The idea behind the *Internet of Things* (Ashton, 2009) was to view physical and digital "things" as having their own identities and physical attributes that are part of a dynamic global infrastructure which enables them to act, interact and communicate between themselves and the environment, triggering all manner of services and providing contextual information when assumed relevant or needed.

Commentators in HCI have also started critiquing the field of HCI from a historical perspective (Bannon, 2011a,b; Grudin, 2012; Hurtienne, 2009). The current era of HCI has been characterized as the third wave (Bødker, 2006) or third paradigm (Harrison et al., 2007). Both are assumed to have replaced the second and earlier first waves/paradigms. Bødker, for example, refers to the first wave of HCI as framing design for the user at a desktop primarily in an office setting; the second wave as a broadening of this to include group working, shaped by ideas about situated and social action together with Scandinavian approaches to participatory design, and the third wave as expanding further into quite new use contexts and application types, that emphasize non-work, non-spaces and non-purposeful engagements, and where notions of culture, emotion, reflexivity and multiple mediation have entered center stage.

Harrison et al. (2011, 2007) have been more forthright in their claims about the third paradigm, arguing that HCI is in a period of crisis and the cluster of alternative approaches currently being articulated and promoted in HCI, such as embodiment, situated construction of meaning, emotion, will become part of a successor science, with "substantially changed epistemological commitments" (p390). They argue that the field needs this kind of Kuhnian shift, making way for multiple analytic perspectives that can expound the experiential quality of interaction and how people make meaning of their contexts and situations when interacting with technologies in their everyday lives.

The idea that we are entering a third wave/paradigm of HCI has struck a chord with many and is becoming part of the HCI discourse (e.g., Taylor, 2011). While strictly not true — since there have not been any *profound* shifts in the ways described by Kuhn (1962) — this rhetoric can help the community to understand the *significant* changes in research direction that have occurred. However, others have argued that alluding to such dramatic paradigmatic shifts in HCI does not reflect what has happened, since Human Factors, Information Processing and other approaches continue to co-exist, serving different purposes in the field (Grudin, 2006). Hence, it is not a case of one wave of research replacing another, but more a question of seeing the evolution of HCI through different epochs that overlap, and in so doing, leading to different questions being asked, methods used and challenges addressed in society's pursuit of ever more technological development (Bannon, 2011b).

Alongside these reflections about the field of HCI, have been debates about whether, how and what kinds of theory can be of value in contributing to the design of new technologies. On the one hand, are staunch advocates, arguing that a theoretical foundation is imperative for addressing the difficult design challenges ahead that face the HCI community (e.g., Barnard et al., 2000; Hollan et al., 2000; Kaptelinin, 1996; Sutcliffe, 2000) but that there is a worrying lack of it (Castell, 2002) echoing earlier concerns about the field that "there is only an HCl theory vacuum" (Long, 1991). On the other hand, some have argue that theory has never been useful for the practical concerns of HCI and that it should be abandoned in favor of continuing to develop more empirically based methods to deal with the uncertain demands of designing quite different user experiences using innovative technologies (e.g., Landauer, 1991). After all, many popular methods, innovative interfaces and design solutions have been developed without a whisker of a theory in sight.

Part of this dilemma has been the acknowledgement that there has been a paucity of adequate theories that can be directly applicable to HCI concerns. It is increasingly acknowledged that theories about human-computer interaction, that were derived from lab-based research often do not map onto the messy human-computer interactions in the real world. People are much more unpredictable — for example, they get distracted and are constantly interrupted or interrupt their own activities by talking to others, taking breaks, starting new activities, resuming others, and so on. Likewise, it has proven difficult to say with any confidence the extent to which a system or particular interface function can be mapped back to a theory. Typically, theories end up as high-level design implications, guidelines or principles in interaction design. The question this raises, therefore, is whether such generalizations — which claim to be based on particular theories — are accurate derivations from those theories. As Kraut (2003) notes, if a system that is designed based on these theories is shown to improve a particular behavior, to what extent can it be said to be due to a specific phenomena identified by a theory? For example, how can we be sure that a computer-based brainstorming tool is responsible for increasing more equitable participation in a meeting because it has reduced social loafing or production blocking? It could be equally due to other factors, such as the time of day, the make-up of the group and so on. It is not surprising, therefore, to often see mixed results, in which sometimes a brainstorming tool has been found to improve a behavior and other times not.

2.4 GROWN-UP HCI: REFRAMING THEORY

Importing and adapting alternative theories from other areas to address new concerns in HCI continues to be a staple of HCI research. Examples include embodied interaction (Dourish, 2001; Hurtienne, 2009), ecological rationality (Todd et al., 2011) and proxemics (Ballendat et al., 2010). Recently, there have been attempts to develop new HCI theories that are based on the body of knowledge accumulating in HCI, as opposed to importing and adapting theories from other disciplines. For example, Rogers (2011) proposes developing new forms of "wild" theory that are based on the findings emerging from recent in-the-wild studies rather than imported theories that are largely derived from lab-based studies. Part of the appeal is their ability to account for technology-augmented behaviors and to inform new interventions to change behaviors that people care about — compared with the scientific theories that were intended to test predictions, and to make generalizations about human performance under controlled conditions. The ones likely to be successful are those that can address a range of interdependencies between design, technology and behavior. But they will need to be framed in the messy world, rather than an idealized world.

In the next chapter, I discuss further the different roles and contributions theory has made to HCI.

CHAPTER 3

The Role and Contribution of Theory in HCI

"Ernest Hilgard used to grumble about psychology that if you develop a theory it's like your tooth-brush, fine for you to use but no one else is very interested in using it." (Jonathan Grudin, 2002).

Theory is very powerful for advancing knowledge in a field. It is the bedrock of many disciplines driving research programs, resulting in insights and enabling new discoveries. A theory can be defined strictly in terms of an explanation of scientific data that follows the scientific method. Predictions are made in terms of hypotheses about an assumed phenomenon, which are then tested, allowing them to be supported because the data cannot be falsified. If the data does not support a hypothesis, it is rejected and the theory is modified and new predictions made.

3.1   INTRODUCTION

Within HCI, the scientific method to theory development was initially adopted as a way of advancing the body of knowledge. However, increasingly other interpretations of theory, drawing from the natural sciences, social sciences, arts and philosophy, have started to be used. These are much broader in scope, where theory is viewed as beginning from description, and then moving onto identification of patterns, and only hundreds of years later, does it become useful theory (Grudin, 2008). Critical theory as viewed in sociology (e.g., Adorno, Habermas), the arts and humanities (e.g., literary theory) and philosophy (e.g., the extended mind theory, Clark, 2004) is not quantifiably measureable, in any scientific sense, but provides conceptual tools and a cogent set of arguments or propositions that can explain or articulate phenomena. Within HCI, a broad church of theory, including those originating in the arts and humanities, is increasingly accepted. A key challenge is finding ways of communicating between the different kinds and levels of theory.

3.2   IMPORTING THEORY

Since the 1980s, HCI has imported numerous kinds of theories, providing the means to analyze and predict the performance of users carrying out tasks for specific kinds of computer interfaces and systems. The theories have been diverse ranging from over-arching theories that attempt to cover the science of HCI — such as Barnard et al.'s (2000) "systems of interactors" intended to bind together contributions from different disciplines — to micro-theories that address a specific phenomenon that can make predictions about certain behaviors — such as dual-task performance — leading to testable hypotheses.

The kinds of theories that have been imported have been primarily cognitive, social and organizational in origin; for example, cognitive theories about human memory have informed the design of interface elements, such as icons, command names and the location of menu items, to make them easy to remember; social psychology theories have informed the design of social experiments which investigate how people communicate and work together in groups when using computer-based collaborative tools and social media; and organizational theories have been developed in CSCW to systematically conceptualize how people interact and process information, make decisions, behave towards others and operate in their work and other social settings (Barley et al., 2004).

One of the main benefits of applying specific theories from other fields about human behavior is they help identify factors (e.g., cognitive, social and organizational) relevant to the design and evaluation of interactive products. In particular, they can help narrow down an area into concerns and research questions that can then be operationalized in terms of a problem or design space. The rationale for selecting a variable or set of variables can be backed up by a proposed cause-effect. For example, the type of words and the syntax that people are likely to remember most with least error may be based on the findings of prior cognitive studies of how subjects learn and recall sets of word-pairings, based on psycholinguistic theory.

3.3   DIFFERENT ROLES AND EXPECTATIONS

Theory works at an abstract level, enabling understandings and generalizations to be made about specific phenomena. Within HCI, a number of vehicles for disseminating these have been proposed, ranging from qualitative and descriptive concepts, themes, patterns, ideas, frameworks, to more formally and predictive, taxonomies, models and principles. They usually are based on assumptions and, at the highest level, aim to provide general laws, rules and formulas, which can be applied in a variety of contexts. The most well known in HCI is Fitt's Law that has been widely used to predict the best placement of buttons and keys on mobile devices and elements on a GUI, to reduce error rate based on the observation of how users aim for targets using their fingers or pointing devices.

An early example of using theory in the scientific tradition was the application of information processing theory to make predictions about how long it would take someone to complete a set of tasks when comparing two or more kinds of interfaces, that varied along one dimension in a controlled way, such as how information was presented (e.g., the efficacy of selecting from 4 menus, each presenting 4 options versus 2 menus, each presenting 8 options). However, as HCI moved from its early roots in engineering through its aspirations to be a scientific discipline to its current mix of science, engineering, art and design, others have argued that the role of theory should be more. Bederson and Shneiderman (2003), for example, suggest that there at least five kinds of theories we should be *aiming* for using in HCI. These are:

- **descriptive** - in the sense of providing concepts, clarifying terminology and guiding further inquiry;

- **explanatory** – in the sense of explicating relationships and processes;

- **predictive** – enabling predictions to be made about user performance;

- **prescriptive** – providing guidance for design;

- **generative** – in the sense of enabling practitioners to create or invent or discover something new.

They suggest that each serves a particular role in the HCI community: *describing* "objects and actions in a consistent and clear manner to enable cooperation" among researchers; *explaining* "processes to support education and training," predicting performance "so as to increase the chances of success;" *prescribing* "guidelines, recommending best practices and cautioning about dangers" to practitioners, and *generating* novel ideas to improve research and practice.

I also discussed the various roles that theory has played in HCI (Rogers, 2004). Some of these overlap with Bederson and Shneiderman's classification, but, in addition, include the following:

- **informative**—selected knowledge and generalizations from another field that provide relevant research findings for HCI to couch understandings and designs;

- **ethnographic**—rich descriptions of a real-world phenomenon interpreted and grounded within a disciplinary tradition, such as anthropology, cognitive science or sociology;

- **conceptual** – the development of high-level frameworks and dimensions for informing and articulating the design and evaluation of prototypes, user interactions and user studies;

- **critical** – critiquing and reasoning about interaction design based on cultural and aesthetic concerns.

Within CSCW, Halverson (2002) also suggested that the role of theory is to provide a conceptual framework that helps the researcher make sense of and describe the world, which can be **descriptive, rhetorical, inferential** or **application-based**. By descriptive, she refers to how a theory can account for a work setting as well as critiquing an implementation of technology in that setting. By rhetorical, she refers to how theory can label important aspects of the conceptual structure that enables researchers to describe things to themselves as well as communicating this to others. By inferential, she refers to engaging in arguments about whether theories are true, or only falsifiable, where sometimes the inferences may be about phenomena that are not fully understood to know where or how to look. By application, she refers to applying theory to the real world for pragmatic reasons, such as informing and guiding system design.

Hence, the role of theory in HCI has been stretched, from how it was originally used as part of the scientific method to being interpreted broadly at different levels to describe, explain, predict and argue with. Whereas in other disciplines, such as chemistry and neuroscience, adhering to the scientific method provides the necessary rigor and criteria to advance knowledge, the widening of theory in HCI has provided many ways of conceptualizing phenomena, in terms of framing, explaining, prescribing and informing — which appears to allow for more transferability. Ultimately, it is an applied field, which means it does not have to be constrained by the restrictions and criteria of a natural science. The downside of such eclecticism, however, is a weakening of its theoretical adequacy, i.e., being certain that an account is representative of the state of affairs.

Many of the early theoretical approaches in HCI followed the scientific tradition, whereby particular theories were used to make predictions about user behavior resulting in prescriptive advice. But as will be discussed in the next chapter their limitations soon became apparent. The emergence of ethnographic approaches in the 1990s was partially as a reaction to this. As an alternative, they offered more expansive ways of accounting for user behavior that was grounded in a particular theoretical or epistemological perspective, including cognitive, social and anthropological ones. A corpus of case studies of the intricate goings on in workplace and other settings appeared (Plowman et al., 1995; Suchman, 1987). They highlighted the importance of considering the social context, the external environment, the artifacts and the interaction and coordination between these during human-computer interactions.

The new kinds of fine-grained, discursive writings were in stark contrast to the concise quantitative results that came out of the predictive and prescriptive approaches to HCI. The accounts of situated human-computer interactions were revelatory, opening many computer scientists' eyes to seeing the world of technology use differently (Dourish, 2001). In turn, it led to thinking about the design and redesign of technologies from very different perspectives. Generative theories then came to the fore that provided design dimensions and constructs to inform the design and selection of new user experiences. More recently, critical theories have provided different ways of understanding, conceptualizing and constructing arguments about aspects of the user experience, interaction design and practice.

3.4   A TAXONOMY OF HCI THEORY: CLASSICAL, MODERN AND CONTEMPORARY

As mentioned in Chapter 1, I have chosen to describe the various theoretical developments in HCI in terms of three periods: Classical, Modern and Contemporary. To reiterate, Classical (Chapter 4) refers to the 1980s, when classical cognitive theories were first imported from cognitive psychology, primarily for modeling and analytic purposes; Modern (Chapter 5) refers to the 1990s and early 2000s when a wide body of theories and frameworks were brought to the field from quite diverse disciplines to address the burgeoning challenges; and Contemporary (Chapter 6) refers to everything that has happened since, including postmodernist, philosophical and in-the-wild approaches.

Classicism in the arts was about setting standards, by being formal and restrained, with a high regard for taste in antiquities. There are parallels in classical HCI, in so far, as rigor and quality of theory were considered central. Similar to the developments in Modern Art, developments in Modern HCI theory were not as prescriptive as in Classical HCI theory. Contemporary HCI is more socially conscious than the previous movements. Theories have been imported and developed with the goal of making an impact on life and a difference to society: including behavioral change, climate change, feminism, multiculturalism, globalization and poverty.

The parallels to art history are meant only as a heuristic, helping to see patterns and commonalities in the scoping and framing of different theories throughout its relatively short history. Others have chosen to link theoretical developments. more closely to the technology eras that have been identified. For example, the turn to the social was not a shift in intellectual thinking but more a recognition that technology and design problems were changing at that time. Similarly, "theories today that focus on place, movement, and ubiquity would still be coffee-time discussions at PARC if we did not have smartphones and other mobile devices" (Carroll, personal communication). If technology development has a strong influence on the choice of theoretical approach, it raises the question of what is in store, post contemporary theories? What theories will we use when computers become increasingly embedded in our bodies, managing our vital organs? But before contemplating where future theories will come from and what role they will play, in the next three chapters, I introduce and discuss the context and theoretical approaches developed in each of the three loosely coined periods.

CHAPTER 4

Classical Theories

In the early 1980s, there was much optimism as to how the field of cognitive psychology could significantly contribute to the development of the field of HCI. A driving force was the realization that most computer systems being developed at the time were difficult to learn, difficult to use and did not enable the users to carry out the tasks in the way they wanted. The body of knowledge, research findings and methods that made up cognitive psychology were seen as providing the means by which to reverse this trend, by being able to inform the design of easy to learn and use computer systems. Much research was carried out to achieve this goal: mainstream information processing theories and models were used as a basis from which to develop design principles, methods, analytic tools and prescriptive advice for the design of computer interfaces (e.g., Carroll, 1991). These are loosely classified into three main approaches: body of knowledge, applying basic research and cognitive modeling (Rogers, 2004). Under the heading cognitive modeling, well-known early conceptual modeling approaches are outlined, including the interface gulfs, GOMS and mental models.

4.1 BODY OF KNOWLEDGE — *Applying existing, of the shelf knowledge*

The most widely known contribution that the field of cognitive psychology made to HCI is the provision of explanations of the capabilities and limitations of users, in terms of what they can and cannot do when performing computer-based tasks. For example, theories that were developed to address key areas, like memory, attention, perception, learning, mental models and decision-making, have been much popularized in tutorials, introductory chapters, articles in magazines and the web to show their relevance to HCI. Popularized examples of this approach included Norman (1988), Preece et al. (1994) and Monk (1984). By explicating user performance in terms of well-known cognitive characteristics that are easy to assimilate (e.g., recognition is better than recall), designers were alerted to their possible effects when making design decisions — something that they might not have otherwise considered.

A well-known example is the application of the finding that people find it easier to recognize things shown to them than to have to recall them from memory. Most graphical interfaces have been designed to provide visual ways of presenting information, that enable the user to scan and recognize an item like a command, rather than require them to recall what command to issue next at the interface.

This approach, however, has tended to be piecemeal — depending on the availability of research findings in cognitive psychology that can be translated into a digestible form. A further problem with this approach is its propensity towards a "jewel in the mud" culture, whereby a single research finding sticks out from the others and is much cited, at the expense of all the other results (Green et al., 1996). In HCI, the "magical number 7+−2" (George Miller's theory about memory, which is that only 7+−2 chunks of information, such as words or numbers, can ever be held in short-term memory at any one time) became the de facto example: nearly every designer had heard of it but not necessarily where it had come from or what situations it is appropriate to apply. A consequence was that it largely devolved into a kind of catchphrase, open to interpretation in all sorts of ways, which ended up being far removed from the original idea underlying the research finding. For example, some designers interpreted the magic number 7+−2 to mean that displays should have no more than 7+−2 of a category (e.g., number of colors, number of icons on a menu bar, number of tabs at the top of a web page and number of bullets in list), regardless of context or task, which is clearly in many cases inappropriate (Bailey, 2000).

4.2   APPLYING BASIC RESEARCH   —or Doing new basic research

A more systematic approach was to select relevant cognitive theories that could be applied to interface design concerns. For example, theories about human memory were used to decide what was the best set of icons or command names to use, given people's memory limitations. One of the main benefits of this approach was to help researchers identify relevant cognitive factors (e.g., categorization strategies, learning methods, perceptual processes) that are important to consider in the design and evaluation of different kinds of GUIs and speech recognition systems. It can also help us understand new kinds of computer-augmented behaviors by examining human's abilities and limitations when interacting with technologies. In particular, the theories demonstrate what humans are good and bad at and, based on this knowledge, can inform the design of technologies that both extend human capabilities and compensate for their weaknesses.

A core lesson that was learned, however, is that you cannot simply lift theories out of an established field (i.e., cognitive psychology), that have been developed to explain specific phenomena about cognition, and then reapply them to explain other kinds of seemingly related phenomena in a different domain (i.e., interacting with computers). This is because the kinds of cognitive processes that are studied in basic research are quite different from what happens in the "real" world of human-computer interactions (Landauer, 1991). In basic research settings, behavior is controlled in a laboratory in an attempt to determine the effects of singled out cognitive processes (e.g., short-term memory span). The processes are studied in isolation and subjects (sic) are asked to perform a specific task, without any distractions or aids at hand. In contrast, the cognition that happens during human-computer interaction is much more messy, whereby many interdependent processes are involved for any given activity. Moreover, in their everyday and work settings, people rarely perform a task in isolation. Instead, they are constantly interrupted or interrupt their own activities, by talking to others, taking breaks, starting new activities, resuming others, and so on. The stark differences between a controlled lab setting and the messy real world setting, meant that many of the theories derived from the former were not applicable to the latter. Predictions based on basic cognitive theories about what kinds of interfaces would be easiest to learn, most memorable, easiest to recognize and so on, were often not supported.

The problem of applying basic research in a real world context is exemplified by the early efforts of a number of cognitive psychologists in the early 1980s, who were interested in finding out what was the most effective set of command names for text editing systems, in terms of being easy to learn and remember. At the time, it was a well-known problem that many users and some programmers had a difficult time remembering the names used in command sets for text editing applications. Several psychologists assumed that research findings on paired-associate learning could be usefully applied to help overcome this problem; this being a well developed area in the basic psychological literature. One of the main findings to be applied was pairs of words are learned more quickly and remembered if subjects have prior knowledge of them (i.e., highly familiar and salient words). It was further suggested that command names be designed to include specific names that have some natural link with the underlying referents they were to be associated with. Based on these hypotheses, a number of experiments were carried out, where users had to learn different sets of command names, that were selected based on their specificity, familiarity, etc. The findings from the studies, however, were inconclusive; some found specific names were better remembered than general terms (Barnard et al., 1982), others showed names selected by users, themselves, were preferable (e.g., Ledgard et al., 1981; Scapin, 1981) while others demonstrated that high-frequency words were better remembered than low-frequency ones (Gunther et al., 1986). Hence, instead of the outcome of the research on command names being able to provide a generalizable design rule about which names are the most effective to learn and remember, it suggested that a whole range of different factors affects the learnability and memorability of command names. As such, the original theory about naming was not able be applied effectively to the selection of optimal names in the context of computer interfaces.

4.3   COGNITIVE MODELING

Another approach that was developed was to model the cognition that is assumed to happen when a user carries out their tasks. Some of the earliest models focused on user's goals and how they could achieve (or not) them with a particular computational system. Most influential at the time were Shneiderman's (1983) framework of direct manipulation (that explicated the properties of graphical user interfaces in terms of continuous representation of objects of interest, and rapid, reversible, incremental actions and feedback enabling a user to directly manipulate objects on the screen, using actions that loosely correspond to those in the physical world), Hutchins et al.'s (1986) conceptual framework of directness (that describes the gap between the user's goals and the way a system works in terms of gulfs of execution and evaluation), and Norman's (1986) theory of action (that models the putative mental and physical stages involved in carrying out an action when using a system). The latter two were heavily influenced by contemporary cognitive science theory of the time, which itself, focused on modeling people's goals and how they were met.

Interface Gulfs in a Nutshell

The idea of there being gulfs at the interface that needed to be bridged was influential in the early theorizing of HCI. Essentially, the gulf of execution and the gulf of evaluation describe the gaps that exist between the user and the interface (Hutchins et al., 1986). They are intended to show how to design the latter to enable the user to cope with them. The first one — the gulf of execution — describes the distance from the user to the physical system while the second one — the gulf of evaluation — is the distance from the physical system to the user (see Figure 4.1). It was proposed that designers and users needed to concern themselves with how to bridge the gulfs in order to reduce the cognitive effort required to perform a task. This could be achieved, on the one hand, by designing usable interfaces that match the psychological characteristics of the user, e.g., taking into account their memory limitations, and, on the other hand, by the user learning to create goals, plans and action sequences that fit with how the interface works.

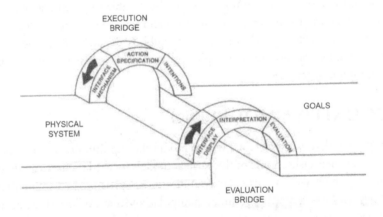

Figure 4.1: Bridging the gulfs of execution and evaluation (from Rogers et al., 2011).

Norman and Hutchins et al.'s respective early cognitive models of the user provided heuristics by which to conceptualize and understand the interactions that were assumed to take place between a user and a system. In so doing, they suggested new ways of thinking about designing interfaces, such as GUIs. In contrast, Card et al.'s (1983) cognitive model of the user, called the model human processor, aimed to be more scientific, by providing a basis from which to make quantitative predictions about user performance and, in so doing, a way of enabling researchers and developers to evaluate different kinds of interfaces in terms of their suitability for supporting various tasks (see Figure 4.2).

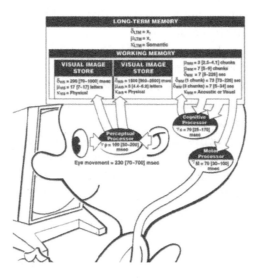

Figure 4.2: The Model Human Processor.

GOMS in a Nutshell

Based upon the established information processing model of the time, Card et al.'s (1983) developed a model of the user, called the model human processor (MHP). It comprised three interacting systems: perceptual, cognitive and motor, each with their own memory and processor. To show how the model could be used to evaluate interactive systems, Card et al. developed a set of predictive models, collectively referred to as GOMS (Goals, Operators, Methods and Selection rules). The resulting suite of methods provided usability engineers with descriptive and analytic tools that were befitting of the engineering approach that was dominant in HCI at the time.

For a while, during the late 1980s and early 1990s, GOMS proved to be highly popular. It was the staple of many courses in HCI and interactive design that started to be run as part of the undergraduate Computer Science curriculum in the U.S. and Europe. Case studies were reported about its success for comparing the efficacy of different computer-based systems (see Olson and Olson, 1991).

The most well-known GOMS success story was Project Ernestine, where a group of researchers carried out a GOMS analysis for a modern workstation that a large phone company were contemplating purchasing, and counter-intuitively, predicted that it would perform worse than the existing computer system being used at the company, for the same kind of tasks. A consequence was that they advised the company not to invest in what could have been potentially a very costly and inefficient technology (Atwood et al., 1996).

While this study has shown that the GOMS approach was useful in helping make purchasing decisions about the effectiveness of new products (although, obviously, they were unable to validate whether if the company had invested in them, it would have been detrimental), it did not take off as a widely used evaluation method. This was due partly to it only being able to model reliably computer-based tasks that involve a small set of highly routine data-entry type tasks. Furthermore, it is intended to be used to predict expert performance, and does not allow for errors to be modeled. This makes it much more difficult (and sometimes impossible) to predict how most users will carry out their tasks when using systems in their work, especially those that have been designed to be flexible in the way they can be used. In most situations the majority of users are highly variable in how they use systems, often carrying out their activities in quite different ways to that modeled or predicted. Many unpredictable factors come into play. These include individual differences among user's, fatigue, mental workload, learning effects and social and organizational factors (Olson and Olson, 1991). Moreover, most people do not carry out their tasks sequentially but tend to be constantly multitasking, dealing with interruptions and talking to others, while carrying out a range of activities.

A problem with using these kinds of predictive models, therefore, is that they can only make predictions about isolated predictable behavior. Given that most people are often unpredictable in the way they behave and, moreover, interweave their ongoing activities in response to unpredictable external demands, it means that the outcome of a GOMS analysis can only ever be a rough approximation.

There have been a number of efforts to make GOMS more usable and applicable to a range of interfaces. Bonnie John has been one of its chief proponents, tirelessly publishing and adapting it for different uses, including CPM-GOMS (John and Gray, 1995) that can model multitasking behavior and CogTool (Teo and John, 2008) that enables non-psychologists to create cognitive models of user tasks from which reliable estimates of skilled user task times can be derived. A number of other cognitive models were developed post GOMS, aimed at predicting user behavior when using various kinds of systems (e.g., the EPIC model, Kieras and Meyer, 1997). Similar to the various versions of GOMS, they can predict simple kinds of user interaction fairly accurately, but are unable to cope with more complex situations, where the amount of judgment a researcher or designer has to make, as to which aspects to model and how to do this, greatly increases (Sutcliffe, 2000). The process becomes increasingly subjective and involves considerable effort, making it more difficult to use them to make predictions that match the ongoing state of affairs.

In contrast, cognitive modeling approaches, that do not have a predictive element to them, have had a wider and more sustained use. Examples include heuristic evaluation (Mohlich and Nielsen,

1990) and cognitive walkthroughs (Polson et al., 1992) that are more widely used by practitioners. Such methods provide various heuristics and questions for evaluators to operationalize and answer, respectively. An example of a well-known heuristic is "minimize user memory load." As such, these more pragmatic methods differ from the other kinds of cognitive modeling techniques insofar as they provide prescriptive advice that is largely based on assumptions about the kinds of cognitive activities users engage in when interacting with a given system.

Mental Models in a Nutshell

Another popular concept that many researchers were attracted by to account for human-computer interactions, but ultimately struggled to explicate adequately, was mental models. The reason the term was so appealing was that it suggested a more dynamic way of characterizing the knowledge that people are assumed to have when interacting with a system, how that enables them to understand how a system works and to know what to do next. However, despite many attempts to capture and unpack the notion of mental models (see Rogers et al., 1992) it was difficult to show they existed and "ran" in the mind as assumed. Just as it has proved to be problematic in cognitive science, to infer the kinds of representations used in the mind it was, likewise, impossible to say with any confidence whether people really developed mental models and if they did, how they functioned in the mind.

In their original instantiation, mental models were postulated as internal constructions of some aspect of the external world that are manipulated, enabling predictions and inferences to be made (Craik, 1943). The process was thought to involve the fleshing out and the running of a mental model (Johnson-Laird, 1983), involving both unconscious and conscious mental processes, where images and analogies were activated. It was argued that the more someone learns about a system and how it functions, the more their mental model develops. For example, appliance engineers have a deep mental model of how home entertainment systems work that allows them to work out how to set them up and fix them. In contrast, an average citizen is likely to have a reasonably good mental model of how to operate their home entertainment system but a shallow mental model of how it works.

Hence, mental models seemed an obvious concept to import into HCI, where a goal was to account for, and, ultimately model how users understand the working of computer systems. An assumption was that if we could tap into this knowledge, we would be able to predict how well people could reason about an interactive system, and provide the necessary training materials, interface types, etc., that would enable them to learn how to use it effectively and know how to troubleshoot if something went wrong at the interface or they made a mistake, and needed to work out how to rectify it.

A number of studies were conducted; people were asked about their knowledge and also observed using devices; many concluded that people's understanding of how computer-based technologies and services, e.g., the Internet, wireless networking, broadband, search engines and viruses, work was alarmingly poor. Norman's earlier assertion (Norman, 1983) that people's mental models are often incomplete, easily confusable, based on inappropriate analogies and superstition was found to be the case. It was discovered that many find it difficult to identify, describe or solve a problem, and lack the words or concepts to explain what is happening.

It was assumed that the situation could be improved if we could find ways of helping users to develop better mental models of interactive systems. Ideally, they should be able to develop a mental model that matched the designer's conceptual model of how they had envisioned the system working. Making the system image more transparent for the users so they could see how it worked and educating them more about how it worked were the two main prescriptive strategies.

The term mental model largely fell into disuse towards the end of the 1990s, as newer theories came to the fore that proposed alternative ways of how people interacted with and understood technologies. These theories moved away from exclusively accounting for the assumed representations inside the head of a user towards explicating a bigger picture of how cognition worked in the world; theories of embodied, distributed and situated action were proposed for how people interacted with the world, with a focus on the artifacts and external representations they use and generate. A major thrust was to unpack interactivity *per se* rather than capturing a putative internal model (Kirsh, 1997); this was more observable and more in line with what users did when using computers. They don't close their eyes to run an internal model in their minds and then open their eyes and apply it to the task in hand. The internal representations that are activated are used in conjunction with the many different forms of external representations, coupled with an array of physical and mental actions, including gesturing, projecting, talking, touching, manipulating, and imagining. As described in the next section, the newer theories provided more scope for inspection and validation — to understand how people make sense of the world around them and the technology they encounter and try to master — than the earlier, more elusive theories of mental models. They also offer more potential for developing generative tools, suggesting how to design interfaces that optimize certain kinds of desired interactivity.

What impact has cognitive modeling had in HCI?

Cognitive modeling approaches made a big impact in the late 1980s and early 1990s, providing techniques for predicting and analyzing users cognitive tasks. The early GOMS family showed how cognitive models could be adapted in HCI. However, models are only ever simplifications of real behavior, and as such, are limited in how and what they capture. So much depends on the researcher's operationalization of human knowledge in terms of putative kinds of internal representations and processes. While these approximations and characterizations enabled them to compare different ways users might perform problem-solving tasks, such as word processing using different operations or searching for information on the web using different browsers, they waned in use in the 1990s when it became more widely recognized that the context of use and external resources and representations were an integral part of the usability of different interfaces.

CHAPTER 5

Modern Theories

In the late 1980s, it became increasingly apparent that the early attempts at importing cognitive psychology theories were failing to live up to their expectations. Several researchers began to reflect on why this was the case, especially why they were unable to be more widely applied to the problems of design and computer use (e.g., Long and Dowell, 1996). There was much navel-gazing, cumulating in the realization that classical cognitive theories were inadequately formulated for informing system design (see Carroll, 1991). A number of problems were identified, including that the theories were too low level, restricted in their scope and failed to deal with real world contexts (Barnard, 1991). The failings of a "one-stream" approach, whereby it was assumed that mainstream theory provided by pure science (i.e., cognitive psychology) could trickle down into the applied science of designing computer systems were exposed (see Long and Dowell, 1996). There was even criticism that psychologists were merely using the field of HCI as a test bed for trying out their general cognitive theories (Bannon and Bødker, 1991) or for validating the assumptions behind specific models (Barnard and May, 1999).

It was still hoped that theory could make a valuable contribution in HCI. The question raised by all this introspection, however, was what kind of theory and what role should it play? Several prominent researchers began to push for other approaches. Long and Dowell (1989, 1996), for example, made persistent calls for more domain-specific theories that could focus on the concerns of users interacting with computers to enable them to work effectively. Carroll et al. (1991) argued that users and designers would benefit more if the process by which tasks and artifacts co-evolved could be "better understood, articulated and critiqued" (p99).

Others revised and adapted their cognitive frameworks to be more representative and build directly on the concerns of HCI (e.g., Draper, 1992). New cognitive theories emerged that focused on interactivity rather than solely modeling what was assumed to happen "inside the head." It was recognized that a more appropriate conceptualization of cognition for HCI was one that was distributed across people, technologies and the environment and externalized. A central focus was the interplay between external representations and internal representations at the interface (e.g., Green et al., 1996; Hutchins, 1995; Kirsh, 1997; Scaife and Rogers, 1996; Wright et al., 2000).

There were also attempts to look for different theories that took into account how the environment affected human action and perception. Several ideas from ecological psychology were imported into HCI (e.g., Gaver, 1991; Norman, 1988). Other researchers began looking elsewhere for theories that were more encompassing, and which could address the concerns of interacting with computers in real-world contexts. By changing the boundaries of what was studied, and by looking at the phenomena of interest with different theoretical lenses and methods, it was assumed that a new set of research questions could be framed, which, in turn, could feed into the design of more usable computer artifacts (Bannon and Bødker, 1991).

Concomitantly, there was a "turn to the social" (Button, 1993): sociologists, anthropologists and others in the social sciences joined HCI, bringing with them new frameworks, theories and ideas about technology use and system design. Human-computer interactions were conceptualized as social phenomena (e.g., Heath and Luff, 1991). Most notable was the situated action (SA) approach and ethnography. A main thrust of the SA approach was to examine the *context* in which users interact with technologies: or put in social terms, how people use their particular circumstances to achieve intelligent action.

The approach known as ethnomethodology (Garfinkel, 1967; Garfinkel and Sacks, 1970) provided much of the conceptual and methodological underpinning for the early ethnography in HCI (Button, 1993). It offered new ways of describing the informal aspects of work, i.e., "the hurly burly of social relations in the workplace and locally specific skills required to perform any task" (Anderson, 1994, p154).

Table 5.1 shows each of the Modern theoretical approaches that are covered, outlining their origins, appropriation in HCI, their impact on research and practice and an "in a nutshell" description. Their selection and amount of coverage is based on their influence in HCI. A section on CSCW theories is also included to show how theory was instrumental in the establishment of that field.

Table 5.1: Modern Theoretical Approaches in HCI

Alternative cognitive approaches

    5.1 External cognition

    5.2 Distributed cognition

    5.3 Ecological psychology

Social approaches

    5.4 Situated action

    5.5 Ethnomethodology and ethnography

    5.6 CSCW theories

Other imported approaches

    5.7 Activity theory

    5.8 Grounded theory

    5.9 Hybrid theories

5.1   EXTERNAL COGNITION

Larkin and Simon's (1987) classic cognitive science paper on why a diagram may be worth a thousand words became a landmark in HCI because it offered the first alternative computational account of cognition which focused on how people interact with external representations. Their seminal idea was that cognition be viewed as the interplay between internal and external representations, rather than only be about modeling what was assumed to happen inside the head. It was regarded by those who had become disaffected by cognitive models as a source of inspiration for rethinking HCI and for me, personally, provided an "aha" moment, leading to the development of a new theory of external cognition (see Rogers, 2008a).

Larkin and Simon's theoretical account made an important distinction between two kinds of external representation: diagrammatic and sentential representations. While being *informationally* equivalent they were considered to be *computationally* different. That is they contain the same information about the problem but the amount of cognitive effort required to come to the solution differed. They proposed that solutions to problems could be "read off" from diagrams that were implicit in sentences. People can readily switch their attention from one component to another in a diagram to draw conclusions in ways that are impossible to do with a sequence of sentences. Diagrams provide simultaneous information about the location of components in a form that enables objects and their relations to be easily tracked and maintained. From this, we can deduce that the best diagrams are those that make it obvious where to look to draw conclusions.

Larkin and Simon's paper paved the way for HCI researchers to begin in earnest to theorize the role of external representations in human-computer interactions. There was a palpable buzz in the early 1990s as they endeavored to change the face of theorizing in HCI. O'Malley and Draper (1992) proposed a display-based account that differentiated between the knowledge users need to internalize when learning to use display-based word processors (e.g., Word) and the knowledge that they can always depend upon being available in the external display. Norman (1993) had a big impact, popularizing the notion that knowledge resides both in "the head" and in "the world." Wright et al. (2000) developed a resource model that analyzed internal (e.g., memorized procedure) and external representations (e.g., written instructions). Kirsh (1997) developed a theory of interactivity that stressed how cognition can be extended in a variety of ways in what we can do, and allowing us to think more powerfully As well as reducing the cognitive effort that is needed to perform tasks, he argued that we should reframe external representations in terms of how they can enhance cognitive power. He suggested a number of ways, including providing a structure that can serve as a shareable object of thought; creating persistent referents; facilitating re-representation and the computation of more explicit encoding of information and helping to coordinate thought. A core aspect of interactivity is the ability to project structure onto things and then modify the world to materialize or reify that projection. People often reorder or rearrange objects in the environment, such as shuffling the letters around in a Scrabble tray to help them work out the best word given their set of letters (Maglio et al., 1999). Kirsh (2010) also stresses how we are always creating external representations; on the one hand they can help reduce memory load and the cognitive cost of computational tasks but, equally, they can do and allow us to think more powerfully.

The theory of external cognition was developed to systematically inform how new technologies, such as animations, multi-media and virtual reality could extend and enhance cognition

(Rogers and Scaife, 1998; Scaife and Rogers, 1996). A number of core dimensions were identified that could be used to guide the design of different kinds of external representations that would be of "added" cognitive value for particular users, domains and tasks. It suggested how interactive mechanisms enabled by computer technologies could be exploited to guide and scaffold learners in knowing where to look in order to interpret, make inferences and connections between the different elements of a graphical representation.

External Cognition in a Nutshell

A central property of external cognition is *computational offloading* — the extent to which different external representations vary the amount of cognitive effort required to carry out different activities (Scaife and Rogers, 1996). This is broken down into specific design dimensions, intended to guide the design of interactive representations. They include *re-representation* (how different external representations, that have the same abstract structure, make problem-solving easier or more difficult) and *graphical constraining* (how elements in a graphical representation are able to constrain the kinds of inferences that can be made about the underlying represented concept). The dimensions were further characterized in terms of design concepts with the purpose of framing questions, issues and trade-offs. Examples of design concepts are *cognitive tracing*, which refers to the way users are allowed to develop their own understanding and external memory of a representation of a topic by being allowed to modify and annotate it; *explicitness* and *visibility* which refers to how to make more salient certain aspects of a display such that they can be perceived and comprehended appropriately. Another design concept is *dynalinking*, which refers to how abstract representations, such as diagrams, are linked together with a more concrete illustration of what they stand for, such as a simulation. Changes in one are matched by changes in the other, enabling a better understanding of what the abstraction means.

The set of external cognition concepts were intended to suggest to designers ways of generating possible functions at the interface. For example, Masterman and Rogers (2002) developed a number of online activities that allowed children to create their own cognitive traces when learning about chronology using an interactive multimedia application. They have also been used for deciding how to design and combine interactive external representations for representing difficult subjects, such as dynamical systems in biology, chronology in history, the working of the cardiac system and crystallography (e.g., Gabrielli et al., 2000; Masterman and Rogers, 2002; Otero, 2003; Price, 2002). Sutcliffe (2000) has also shown how he used the theory to inform the design of multimedia explanations. The approach was also applied in work settings, to inform the design of online graphical representations that could facilitate and support complex distributed problem solving (Rodden et al., 2003; Scaife et al., 2002). Dynalinking has been used in a number of areas to explicitly show relationships among multiple dimensions where the information to be understood or learned is complex (Sutcliffe, 2000). For example, it has been used to represent complex data using various interactive visualizations, for domains like learning science subjects, economic forecasting, molecular modeling, and statistical analyses.

Other analytic frameworks that were developed under the umbrella of the external cognition approach include Green's (1989) cognitive dimensions and Wright et al.'s (2000) resource model.

5.1.1   COGNITIVE DIMENSIONS

Cognitive dimensions were intended to enable psychologists and importantly, designers, to make sense of and use when talking together about design issues. Green's overarching goal was to develop a set of high-level concepts that were both valuable and easy to use for evaluating the designs and assessment of informational artifacts, such as software applications. An example dimension is "viscosity," which simply refers to resistance to local change. The analogy of stirring a spoon in treacle (high viscosity) versus milk (low viscosity) quickly gives the idea. Having understood the concept in a familiar context, Green then showed how the dimension could be further explored to describe the various aspects of interacting with the information structure of a software application. In a nutshell, the concept is used to examine "how much work you have to do if you change your mind" (Green, 1990, p79). Different kinds of viscosity were described, such as "knock-on' viscosity," where performing one goal-related action makes necessary the performance of a whole train of extraneous actions. The reason for this is due to constraint density: the new structure that results from performing the first action violates some constraint, which must be rectified by the second action, which in turn leads to a different violation, and so on. An example is editing a document using a word processor without widow control. The action of inserting a sentence at the beginning of the document can have a knock-on effect whereby the user must then go through the rest of the document to check that all the headers and bodies of text still lie on the same page.

The approach was meant to be broad-brush, and importantly, comprehensible to and usable by non-specialists. The original set of terms comprised a small vocabulary of about 12 terms that describe aspects of user interaction that are cognitively relevant. Besides viscosity, they included premature commitment ("are there strong constraints in terms of the order of how tasks are to be carried out?"), diffuseness ("how much space does the notation require to produce a certain result or express a meaning?") and visibility ("how readily can required parts of the notation be identified, accessed and made visible?"). Some are more intuitive to understand than others. One of Green's claims about the value of cognitive dimensions is that by identifying different kinds of dimensions at a suitable level of abstraction across applications, solutions found in one domain may be applicable to similar problems found in others.

Although never widely used, the lingua franca of "cog dims" has been influential. In particular, it has been used to determine why some interfaces are more effective than others. These include educational multimedia (e.g., Oliver, 1997; Price, 2002), collaborative writing (Woods, 1995), tangible user interfaces (Edge and Blackwell, 2006) and programming environments (Modugno et al., 1994; Yang et al., 1995). Kadoda et al. (1999) and Blackwell and Green (2000) also extended the approach by developing a generalized questionnaire in which the definitions of cog dims are provided for users rather than designers, who decide for themselves the features of a system that they wish to criticize. Designers and researchers who have been exposed to them for the first time have found them comprehensible, requiring not too much effort to understand and to learn how to use (Green et al., 1996). Indeed, when one first encounters the cog dims there is a certain quality about them that lends to articulation. They invite one to consider explicitly trade-offs in design solutions that might otherwise go unnoticed and which, importantly, can be traced to the cognitive phenomena they are derived from.

5.1.2   WRIGHT ET AL.'S RESOURCES MODEL

Wright et al. (2000) modeled external cognition in terms of *resources* that are drawn upon during user interaction. They categorized these in terms of plans, goals, possibilities, history, actions-effect relations or states. They could be represented internally (e.g., memorized procedure) or externally (e.g., written instructions). Configurations of these resources, distributed across internal and external representations, were assumed to be what informs an action. In addition, the way the resources are configured in the first place, is assumed to come about through various "interaction strategies." These include things like plan following and goal matching. Thus, a user's selection of a given action may arise through an internal goal matching strategy (e.g., delete the file) being activated in conjunction with an external "cause-effect relation" being perceived, (e.g., a dialog box popping up on the screen saying 'are you sure you want to delete this file?').

Wright et al.'s (2000) analytic framework identified patterns of interaction together with the variability of resources that are used at different stages of a task — such as determining when a user can depend on the external resources (e.g., action-effect relations) to constrain what to do next and when they must rely more on their own internal resources (e.g., plans, goals and history of actions). The idea was that the analyst could reflect on the problems with a given interface in terms of the demands the various patterns of resources place on the user.

What impact has external cognition had on HCI?

One of the main uses of the external cognition approach in HCI has been to enable researchers and designers to articulate designs and phenomena in terms of a set of core properties and design dimensions — which they did not have access to before. In so doing, a language, couched in how people manipulate representations, interact with objects, etc., at an interface, was provided, helping researchers to select, articulate and validate particular forms of external representation in terms of how they could support various activities being designed for. Besides the originators of the theoretical frameworks, they have been used by a number of others to inform the design of various interfaces. Their emphasis on determining the optimal way of structuring and presenting interactive content with respect to the cognitive effort involved can be viewed as being generative Although largely superseded by contemporary theories that address a broader range of user aspects, the extended cognition approach still has much to offer in terms of helping designers select and create interactive visualizations, feedback and multi-modal representations.

5.2   DISTRIBUTED COGNITION

The distributed cognition approach considers cognitive phenomena in terms of individuals, artifacts, and internal and external representations (Hutchins, 1995). It provides a more extensive account compared with external cognition. Typically, it involves describing a "cognitive system," which entails interactions among people, the artifacts they use, and the environment they are working in. It was initially developed by Hutchins and his colleagues in the late 1980s and proposed as a radically new paradigm for rethinking all domains of cognition (Hutchins, 1995). It was argued that what was problematic with the classical cognitive science approach was not its conceptual framework *per se,* but its exclusive focus on modeling the cognitive processes that occurred within one individual. Alternatively, Hutchins argued that what was needed was for the same conceptual framework to be applied to a range of cognitive systems, including socio-technical systems at large (i.e., groups of individual agents interacting with each other in a particular environment).

Part of the rationale for this extension was that, firstly, it was assumed to be easier and more accurate to determine the processes and properties of an "external" system — since they can arguably, to a large extent, be observed directly in ways not possible inside a person's head — and, secondly, they may actually be different and thus unable to be reduced to the cognitive properties of an individual. To reveal the properties and processes of a cognitive system requires doing an ethnographic field study of the setting and paying close attention to the activities of people and their interactions with material media (Hutchins, 1995). These are conceptualized in terms of "internal and external representational structures" (Hutchins, 1995, p135). It also involves examining how information is propagated through different media in the bounded cognitive system.

Distributed Cognition in a Nutshell

The distributed cognition approach provides an event-driven description of the information and its propagation through a cognitive system. The cognitive system might be one person's use of a computational tool, such as a calculator; two people's joint activities when designing the layout for the front page of a newspaper, using a shared authoring tool, or more widely, a large team of software developers and programmers, examining how they coordinate their work with one another, using a variety of mediating artifacts, such as schedules, clocks, to-do lists and shared files.

The granularity of analysis varies depending on the activities and cognitive system being observed and the research or design questions being asked. For example, if the goal is to examine how a team of pilots fly a plane — with a view to improving communication between them — then the focus will be on the interactions and communications that take place between them and their instruments, at a fine level of granularity. If the goal is to understand how pilots learn how to fly — with a view to developing new training materials — then the focus will be at a coarser grain of analysis, taking into account the cultural, historical, and learning aspects involved in becoming a pilot.

The description produced may cover a period of a day, an hour or only minutes, depending on the study's focus. For the longer periods, verbal descriptions are primarily used. For the shorter periods, micro-level analyses of the cognitive processes are meticulously plotted using diagrammatic forms and other graphical representations. The rationale for performing the finer levels of analysis is to reveal practices and discrepancies that would go unnoticed using coarser grains of analysis, but which reveal themselves as critical to the work activity. A distributed cognition analysis typically involves examining:

- The distributed problem-solving that takes place (including the way people work together to solve a problem).
- The role of verbal and non-verbal behavior (including what is said, what is implied by glances, winks, etc. and what is not said).
- The various coordinating mechanisms that are used, e.g., rules, procedures.
- The various ways communication takes place as the collaborative activity progresses.

- How knowledge is shared and accessed.

It should be stressed that there isn't one single way of doing a distributed cognition analysis. Within work settings, data is collected and then analyzed and interpreted in terms of work practices, routines and procedures followed, and the work arounds that teams develop when coping with the various demands placed upon them at different times during their work. Breakdowns, incidents or unusual happenings are highlighted, especially where it is discovered that excessive time is being spent doing something, errors were made using a system, or a piece of information was passed on incorrectly to someone else or misheard.

Problems can also be described in terms of the communication pathways that are being hindered or the breakdowns arising due to information not propagating effectively from one representational state to another. This level of analysis can reveal where information is being distorted, resulting in poor communication or inefficiency. Conversely, it can show when different technologies and the representations displayed via them are effective at mediating certain work activities and how well they are coordinated.

Hutchins emphasizes that an important part of doing a distributed cognition analysis is to have a deep understanding of the work domain that is being studied. He recommends, where possible, that the investigators learn the trade under study. This can take a team of researchers several months and even years to accomplish and in most cases this is impractical for a research or design team to do. Alternatively, it is possible to spend a few weeks immersed in the culture and setting of a specific team to learn enough about the organization and its work practices to conduct a focused analysis of a particular cognitive system.

The distributed cognition approach has been used primarily by researchers to analyze a variety of cognitive systems, including airline cockpits (Hutchins and Klausen, 1996; Hutchins and Palen, 1997), air traffic control (Halverson, 1995), call centers (Ackerman and Halverson, 1998), software teams (Flor and Hutchins, 1992), control systems (Garbis and Waern, 1999), emergency rooms (Artman and Waern, 1999), emergency medical dispatch (Furniss and Blandford, 2006) and engineering practice (Rogers, 1993, 1994). One of the main outcomes of the distributed cognition approach is an explication of the complex interdependencies between people and artifacts in their work activities. An important part of the analysis is identifying the problems, breakdowns and the distributed problem-solving processes that emerge to deal with them. In so doing, it provides multi-level accounts, weaving together "the data, the actions, the interpretations (from the analyst), and the ethnographic grounding as they are needed" (Hutchins and Klausen, 1996, p19). For example, Hutchins' account of ship navigation provides several interdependent levels of explanation, including how navigation is performed by a team on the bridge of a ship; what and how navigational tools are used, how information about the position of the ship is propagated and transformed through the different media and the tools that are used.

As a theoretical approach, it has received considerable attention from researchers in the cognitive and social sciences, most being very favorable. However, there have been criticisms of the approach, mainly as a continuation of an ongoing objection to cognitive science as a valid field of study and, in particular, the very notion of cognition (e.g., Button, 1997). In terms of its application in HCI, Nardi (1996, 2002) has voiced her concerns about its utility in HCI. Her main criticism stems from the need to do extensive fieldwork before being able to come to any conclusions or design decisions for a given work setting. Furthermore, she points out that there is not a set of interlinked concepts that can be readily used to pull things out from the data. In this sense, Nardi has a point: the distributed cognition approach is difficult to apply, since there is not a set of explicit features to be looking for, nor is there a check-list or recipe that can be easily followed when doing the analysis. It requires a high level of skill to move between different levels of analysis, to be able to dovetail between the detail and the abstract. As such it can never be viewed as a "quick and dirty" prescriptive method. The emphasis on doing (and interpreting) ethnographic fieldwork to understand a domain means that at the very least, considerable time, effort and skill is required to carry out an analysis.

Where the distributed cognition framework can be usefully applied to design concerns, is in providing a detailed level of analysis which can provide several pointers as to how to change a design (especially forms of representation) to improve user performance, or, more generally, a work practice. For example, Halverson (2002) discusses how in carrying out a detailed level of analysis of the representational states and processes involved at a call center, she was, firstly, able to identify why there were problems of coordination and, secondly, determine how the media used could be altered to change the representational states to be more optimal. Hence, design solutions can start to emerge from a detailed level of analysis because the nature of the descriptions of the cognitive system is at the same level as the proposed design. In other words, the low-level nature of a distributed cognition analysis can be most useful at revealing the necessary information to know how to change a design, when it has been identified as being problematic.

There have also been various efforts to develop more applied distributed cognition methods that are more accessible and easier to apply. One in particular that has been used by a number of researchers is Distributed Cognition for Teamwork (DiCoT) — essentially a structured approach for analyzing work systems and teamwork (Blandford and Furniss, 2005; Furniss and Blandford, 2010). The approach draws on core ideas from DC theory and combines them with more practical aspects of contextual design (Beyer and Holtzblatt, 1998; Holtzblatt and Jones, 1993), that resulted in a comprehensive set of underlying themes and principles intended to guide researchers in knowing what to focus on when analyzing and interpreting data from workplace settings. Themes include physical layout, information flow, and the design and use of artifacts; principles include subtle bodily supports (for example, pointing on a screen while replying to someone who walks in and asks a question is part of the mechanism of remembering where they are in a task) and arrangement of equipment (e.g., where computers, printers, etc., are in an office determines who has access to and can interact with information). The themes and principles are intended to help researchers organize their field observations into a set of interdependent models that can help elicit insights about user behavior.

Contextual design

Contextual design (Beyer and Holtzblatt, 1998) is not a theory but an applied approach that was developed to deal with the collection and interpretation of ethnographic findings. It is only briefly mentioned here because it was an important component in the development of the applied DiCoT framework. It is concerned with explicating context and the social aspects of user-interaction and how to use this to inform the design of software. It focuses on how to progress layers of abstractions rather than bridging analysis and design through examining the detail of each. It is also much more prescriptive, promoting a process of transforming data into a set of abstractions and models. The outcome is a very hands-on method of applying research findings, that has proven to be highly successful, with many other practitioners having adopted and used it. Part of its attraction lies in its conceptual scaffolding; it offers a step-by-step approach with various forms to fill in and use to transform findings into more formal structures.

A benefit of bringing together the various strands of the DC literature is to provide a more structured framework that can help researchers and developers to identify the strengths and limitations of the current artifact designs. In so doing, it should enable them to reason systematically about how to re-design the work settings, in terms of considering new technologies, work practices, physical layout, etc. Others have also started to use it to analyze work practices, including software team interactions (Sharp and Robinson, 2008) and mobile healthcare settings (McKnight and Doherty, 2008).

What impact has the distributed cognition approach had on HCI?

The distributed cognition approach has been widely used in HCI to analyze existing practices and to inform new and redesigns by examining how the form and variety of media in which information is currently represented might be transformed and what might be the consequences of this for a work practice. Partially in response to the criticism leveled at the difficulty of applying the distributed cognition approach, Hutchins and his colleagues (Hollan et al., 2000) set an agenda for how it could be used more widely within the context of HCI. They proposed it was well suited both to understanding the complex networked world of information and computer-mediated interactions and for informing the design of digital work materials and collaborative work places. They suggested a comprehensive methodological framework for achieving this.

Conducting a detailed distributed cognition analysis and using the DiCoT method has enabled researchers and designers to explore the trade-offs and likely outcomes of potential solutions and in so doing suggest a set of requirements grounded in the details of the work place, e.g., types of information resources, that are considered suitable for specific kinds of activities. The way theory has been applied from the DC approach has been largely descriptive and, to a lesser extent, generative; providing a detailed articulation of a cognitive system, and in so doing, providing the basis from which to generate design solutions.

5.3   ECOLOGICAL PSYCHOLOGY

The ecological psychology approach — originally developed by Gibson (1966, 1979) — was also considered by several researchers to be more relevant to HCI than the classical cognitive theories, especially for addressing how users interacted with the external world. For Bill Gaver (2008), reading Gibson was a revelation; making a huge impact on his thinking and convincing him of the importance of *contextualizing* human computer interactions in the environment they occur in rather than following the mainstream cognitive approach of isolating and identifying representations solely in the head.

Gibson's view was that psychology should be the study of the interaction between humans and their environment. This involved describing in detail the environment and people's ordinary activities within it (Neisser, 1985). HCI researchers took his philosophy and insights to heart, adapting his concepts in order to examine how people interacted with technological artifacts (Gaver, 1991; Kirsh, 2001; Norman, 1988; Rasmussen and Rouse, 1981; Vicente, 1995; Woods, 1995).

Ecological Psychology in a Nutshell

A central part of Gibson's ecological psychology theory is the notion of invariant structures in the environment and how they relate to human perception and action. Two that were considered most relevant to HCI were *ecological constraints* and *affordances*. Ecological constraints refer to structures in the external world that guide people's actions rather than those that are determined by internal cognitive processes. An affordance refers to the relationship between the properties of a person and the perceptual properties of an object in the environment. Within the context of HCI, it is used to refer to attributes of objects that allow people to know how to use them. In a nutshell, to afford is taken to mean "to give a clue" (Norman, 1988). Specifically, when the affordances of an object are perceptually obvious it is assumed that they make it easy to know how to interact with the object (e.g., door handles afford pulling, cup handles afford grasping). Norman (1988) provided a range of examples of affordances associated with everyday objects such as doors and switches — that were easy to understand and use when talking about interfaces.

This explication of affordances in HCI is simpler than Gibson's original idea — and to some extent that has been part of its appeal. It rapidly came into widespread use in HCI providing a way for researchers and designers, alike, to describe interfaces, suggesting to the user what to do when carrying out a task. It provided them with an easy to use shared articulatory device, helping them think about how to represent objects at the interface that could readily afford permissible actions (Gaver, 1991) and providing cues as to how to interact with interface objects more easily and efficiently.

It is not necessary to know about the original ecological psychology theory to understand the concepts that have been imported into HCI. Instead, the idea of invariant structures is taken as a given. The problem of only having a shallow understanding of an affordance, however, is that it requires working out what are affordable objects at the interface (St. Amant, 1999). There are no abstractions, methods, rules or guidelines to help the researcher identify instances of something — only analogies drawn from the real world.

Indeed, many designers began to use the term affordances to apply to everything, and as a way of thinking and talking about what adding a feature to the interface might mean to the user. It became easy to slip into talking about the meaning of an icon, the way a scroll bar moved, and the positioning of a window — as being easy to understand, because they afforded clicking on. Norman, however, was horrified at how sloppily the term had become used in common design parlance. To better articulate how to use the notion of affordances at the interface, he thought it important to understand the distinction between two kinds: perceived and real (Norman, 1999). On the one hand, physical objects were considered to have real affordances, as described above, like grasping, which are perceptually obvious and do not have to be learned. User interfaces that are screen-based, on the other hand, do not have these kinds of real affordances. Importantly, this means that users have to learn the meaning and function of each object represented at the interface before knowing how to act. Norman argued that screen-based interfaces have perceived affordances, which are based on learned conventions and feedback. For example, having a red flashing button icon appear at the interface may provide visual cues to enable the user to perceive that clicking on that icon is a meaningful useful action at that given time in their interaction with the system, that has a known outcome.

Vicente (1995) and Vicente and Rasmussen's (1990) considered it more beneficial to import more of the original theory into HCI, and so developed the Ecological Interface Design framework. Affordances were described in terms of a number of actions (e.g., moving, cutting, throwing, carrying). The various actions are sorted into a hierarchy of categories, based on what, why and how they afford. The framework was intended to allow designers to analyze a system at different levels, which correspond to the levels in the hierarchy.

Kirsh (2001) also proposed operationalizing the notion of affordance by grounding it more in the original Gibsonian ideas. Instead of couching it in terms of objects giving clues as to what to do, he proposed viewing affordance in terms of structures in the environment that *invite* people to do something. The term he used was *entry points*. Consider the way information is laid out on posters, websites and magazines; they provide different entry points for scanning, reading and following. These include headlines, columns, pictures, cartoons, figures, tables and icons. Well-designed information allows a person's attention to move rapidly from entry point to entry point for different sections (e.g., menu options, lists, descriptions). Poorly designed information does not have clear entry points — it is hard to find things. In Kirsh's terms, entry points are affordances in the sense of inviting people to carry out an activity (e.g., read it, scan it, look at it, listen to it, click on it). This reconceptualization potentially has more design purchase as it encourages designers to think about the coordination and sequencing of actions and the kind of feedback to provide, in relation to how objects are positioned and structured at an interface — rather than simply whether an object *per se* suggests what to do with them.

The concept of entry points has since been used successfully in interaction design as a design and conceptual tool. For example, Lidwell et al. (2006) have operationalized it as a generative design principle, describing features that, on the one hand, lure people into them and, on the other, do not deter them from entering them. Rogers et al. (2009) used entry points as the basis of their Shared Information Spaces framework, which was intended for researchers to think about how to constrain or invite group participation and collaboration through the layout of a physical room, the display and device interfaces provided and the kind and way information is presented (physical or digital). The assumption is that the design of entry points can provide different ways for participants to collaborate in both verbal and physical modes that lend themselves to more or less equitable participation. Hornecker et al. (2007) have also incorporated entry points into their comprehensive framework on the shareability of devices. The framework also includes other concepts such as access points, overview and fluidity of sharing, which are intended to show the relationship between elements of space, technology and people, by denoting design characteristics that invite people into engagement with a group activity and entice them to interact and join a group's activity. The assumption is that considering the relationship between the various elements in the framework can encourage a more comparative approach to designing interfaces for shared use. In so doing, it can enable a number of more specific research questions and hypotheses to be generated that could be investigated experimentally.

What impact has ecological psychology had on HCI?

A main contribution of the ecological psychology approach in HCI has been to extend its discourse, primarily in terms of articulating certain properties about an interface or space in terms of their behavior, appearance and properties. As such the role of theory is largely descriptive, providing design concepts. Most significantly, it has generated core terms that have become part of interaction design's everyday parlance, namely affordance and entry points.

5.4   SITUATED ACTION

The turn "to the social" took place in the late 1980s and early 1990s as a reaction against the dominant cognitive paradigm in HCI. During that time, several sociologists proposed alternative approaches for analyzing user-interaction (see Button, 2003; Shapiro, 1994) that focused on the social aspects of work settings and technology support. Lucy Suchman's (1987) book *Plans and Situated Action* took the field by storm and was universally read by all in HCI; its impact was to have a profound effect on how computation, programming, users and interface design were construed and researched. As well as providing an indisputable critique of the classical cognitive approaches, her alternative ideas about situated action resonated with many who had become disaffected with information-processing models underlying much of HCI.

The situated action *approach* has its origins in cultural anthropology. Suchman (1987) argued for "accounts of relations among people, and between people and the historically and culturally constituted worlds that they inhabit" (p71). To achieve this requires examining the relationship between "structures of action and the resources and constraints afforded by physical and social circumstances" (p179). This involves analyzing "how people use their circumstances to achieve intelligent action (...) rather than attempting to abstract action away from its circumstances" (p50). Suchman was quite clear in her intentions not to produce formal models of knowledge and action, but to explore the relationship of knowledge and action to the specific circumstances in which knowing and acting happen.

Situated Action in a Nutshell

The situated action approach offers detailed accounts of how technology is used by people in different contexts, which can often be quite different from the way the technology was intended to be used. The method used to reveal these discrepancies is predominantly ethnographic (i.e., carrying out extensive observations, interviews, collecting video and note taking of a particular setting). Typically, the findings are contrasted with the prescribed way of doing things, i.e., how people ought to be using technology given the way it has been designed. Sometimes conversational analysis (CA) is used to interpret the dialogue and interactions that take place between users and machine. For example, one of the earliest studies, using this approach was Suchman's (1983) critique of office procedures in relation to the design of office technology. Her analysis showed how there is a big mismatch between how work is organized in the process of accomplishing it in a particular office and the idealized models of how people should follow procedures that underlie the design of office technology. Simply, people do not act or interact with technology in the way prescribed by these kinds of models. Instead, Suchman argued that designers would be much better positioned to design systems that could match the way people behave and use technology if they began by considering the actual details of a work practice. The benefits of doing so could then lead to the design of systems that are much more suited to the kinds of interpretative and problem-solving work that are central to office work.

In Suchman's (1987) much-cited study — of how pairs of users interacted with an expert help system, intended as a help facility for using with a photocopier — she stressed how the design of such systems would greatly benefit from analyses that focus on the unique details of the user's particular situation — rather than any preconceived models of how people ought (and will) follow instructions and procedures. Her detailed analysis of how the expert help system was unable to help users in many situations where they got stuck highlighted again the inadequacy of basing the design of an interactive system primarily on an abstract user model. In particular, her findings showed how novice users couldn't follow the procedures, as anticipated by the user model, but instead engaged in ongoing, situated interaction with the machine with respect to what they considered at that moment as an appropriate next action.

SA analyses have revealed that while people may have plans of action in mind, they often need to change them depending on what is actually happening in a specific situation. They use their embodied and past experiences to deal with the contingencies of the ongoing situation. The canonical example provided by Suchman (1987) is of someone going over the falls in a canoe.

"In planning to run a series of rapids in a canoe, one is very likely to sit for a while above the falls and plan one's decent. The plan might go something like "I'll get as far over to the left as possible, try to make it between those two large rocks, then back very hard to the right to make it around that next bunch." A great deal of deliberation, discussion, simulation, and reconstruction may go into such a plan. But however detailed, the plan stops short of the actual business of getting your canoe through the falls. When it really comes down to the details of responding to currents and handling a canoe, you effectively abandon the plan and fall back on whatever embodied skills are available to you."

Following Suchman, a number of field studies were published that explored the situated and social aspects of user interaction in the work contexts they occurred. The outcome was a corpus of detailed "thick" accounts of a diversity of work practices and based on these design guidance about the specifics of the setting studied (Plowman et al., 1995). However, a criticism leveled at the situated action approach is its focus on the "particulars" of a given setting, making it difficult to step back and generalize. For example, Nardi (1996) exclaims how in reading about the minutiae of a particular field study "one finds oneself in a claustrophobic thicket of descriptive detail, lacking concepts with which to compare and generalize" (p92). This suggests it can be difficult for those used to seeing the world in abstractions to conceptualise it at such a level of detail. In an attempt to overcome this limitation, Hughes et al. (1997) proposed a generalizable framework to help structure the presentation of ethnographic findings in a way that was intended to act as a bridge between fieldwork and "emerging design decisions." The abstractions are discussed in terms of three core dimensions intended to orient the designer to thinking about particular design problems and concerns in a focused way, that in turn can help them articulate why a solution might be particularly helpful or supportive. These are "Distributed Coordination" (work tasks are performed as patterns of activity, e.g., division of labor), "plans and procedures" (the organizational support for distributed coordination, such as project plans and schedules, job descriptions) and "awareness of work" (the organization of work activities that makes them "visible" to others doing the work).

What impact has the situated action approach had in HCI?

The influence of the situated action approach on HCI practice has been pervasive. Suchman became one of the most frequently cited authors in the HCI literature. It changed the way researchers thought of computer interactions and work activities, taking context to be a focal concern. Several researchers reported how the situated action approach has profoundly changed the way they think about how they conceptualise and develop system architectures and interface design (e.g., Button and Dourish, 1996; Clancey, 1993). The situated approach has also become part of designer's talk; concepts of "situatedness" and "context" often being mentioned as important to design for. Hence, the situated action approach has, arguably, had a considerable influence on designers. Nowadays, it is increasingly common for designers and others to spend time "in the field" understanding the context and situation they are designing for before proposing design solutions (Bly, 1997).

Its contribution is descriptive, providing accounts of working practices. It has also had a big impact in the field , facilitating the widespread use of socially oriented concepts, such as context, and inspiring the development of analytic frameworks.

5.5   ETHNOMETHODOLOGY AND ETHNOGRAPHY

Another significant contribution to the "turn to the social" was ethnomethodologically informed ethnography, where field studies were conducted of work practices and interpreted in terms of the practical accomplishment of the people involved (Anderson, 1994). Similar to the situated action approach, it was developed in HCI as a reaction against mainstream cognitive theories. As the name suggests, it is considered an approach to adopt within HCI rather than a theory *per se*.

Ethnomethodology was originally proposed as an alternative *methodology* in sociology, intended to replace traditional top-down theories that sought to identify invariant structures (Garfinkel, 1967; Garfinkel and Sacks, 1970). Such external points of view of the world were considered not at all representative of the actual state of affairs. In this sense, it has an anti-theoretical stance, being quite explicit about its epistemological origins.

Ethnomethodology in a Nutshell

Ethnomethodology is concerned with how people accomplish social order in their everyday and work settings. Social order refers to the interactional work through which people conduct themselves (Garfinkel, 2002). This is viewed as an accomplishment in how society's members craft their moment-to-moment interaction. Essentially, it views people as shaping their actions rather than their actions being shaped by their environment. Ethnographic data is collected and analyzed to reveal how this is achieved. The accounts of work practices are presented largely as thick descriptions (Geertz, 1993). By this it is meant extensive and very detailed accounts.

Within HCI, the ethnomethodological approach has provided illuminating accounts of the details of work practices through which actions and inter-actions are achieved. Hence, it is an approach rather than a theory. It was popularized mainly by British sociologists, who used it to analyze a number of workplace settings; the most well known were of a control center in the London Underground (Heath and Luff, 1991) and of air traffic control (Bentley et al., 1992). They can be very revealing, often exposing taken for granted working practices, which turn out to be central to the efficacy of how a technological system is being used in a setting.

They have also been used to evaluate a number of technology designs and interventions, including Heath and Luff's series of studies on media spaces, augmented paper and hospital equipment (cited in Button, 2003). A recent study of theirs has also used it, first, to examine the interactional and sequential organization of museum visitor's actions and second, based on the findings, to inform the design of the conduct of a robot guide (Yamazaki et al., 2009). The robot guide was provided with various resources to engage visitors when interacting with a particular art exhibit. An evaluation of the robot *in situ* revealed how these resources were useful in engaging visitors in explanations.

A tension ethnomethodologists have had to confront, when working in HCI, is to show how their accounts can be useful for the design of technology and work. To begin, there was an expectation that the rich descriptions would lend themselves to being translated into "design implications" and several, started to add them at the end of their descriptions of field studies. The problem of asking ethnomethodologists to venture into this unfamiliar territory — namely, offering advice for others to follow — however, is that it forces them to come up with a cursory set of bullet points (Rogers, 1997). Many felt uncomfortable offering advice to others, whose very profession is to design — which clearly theirs is not. Their role is regarded as descriptive not prescriptive (Cooper, 1991). By bowing to such pressure, the design guidance ended up being rather tokenistic and not in keeping with the rich descriptions. For example, in one study, Anderson et al. (1993) provided a very detailed and insightful descriptive account of an organization's working practice. Following this, they outlined four brief "bullet-point" guidelines. One of these is that designers need support tools that take up a minimal amount of their time and that such tools should be adaptive to the exigencies of changing priorities. Such an observation is stating the obvious and could have easily been recognized without the need of a detailed field study. It is not surprising, therefore, that this form of abstracting from detailed field studies opened itself up for criticism; "most designers know the former only too well and desire the latter only too much" (Rogers, 1997, p68).

Recognizing this as a dilemma resulted in rethinking what else could be offered besides bullet points tacked on the end of thick descriptions. As one alternative, Button and Dourish (1996) proposed a core set of social mechanisms that had been proposed by the founders of ethnomethodology. These included the higher order concepts of practical action, order, accountability and coordination. Furthermore, they argued that ethnomethodologists and interaction designers could benefit by trying to see the world through each other's perspective: "design should adopt the analytic mentality of ethnomethodology, and ethnomethodology should don the practical mantle of design" (p22). It was suggested that this form of synergism could be achieved through system design taking on board concepts, such as situatedness, practical action, order and accountability, while ethnomethodology could benefit from taking on board system design concepts like generalization, configuration, data and process and mutability. While this approach was a laudable attempt at pushing a new dialogue in HCI it never took off. This is partly because the concepts were too difficult to define, appropriate and use in the different contexts.

Besides ethnomethodological-ethnography, a number of other ethnographic field studies have been published in the HCI and CSCW literature. Their theoretical and analytic framings vary; some being anthropological ethnography, focusing on cultural aspects, and others being cognitive ethnography, using concepts from distributed cognition to frame research questions and explain their data. Such eclecticism is considered by most to be healthy for the field, providing multiple perspectives and ways of understanding a diversity of human computer interactions, besides only being viewed from an ethnomethodology stance. However, at a recent CHI conference, a controversial paper surfaced, arguing that there was only really one acceptable way of grounding ethnography in HCI, namely in ethnomethodology (Crabtree et al., 2009). Much criticism was pitted against the new ethnographies that have been published on everyday settings, and which are not concerned with systems design *per se*. Crabtree et al.'s beef with the new ethnographies is in the "methodological dangers" that might arise when switching the focus to cultural practice; the ensuing accounts become more of a *literary practice* (Crabtree et al.'s emphasis) where design ideas are based on "conceptual rhetoric" rather than on the "organized conduct of those who will ultimately use the technology." Compared with the rich descriptions that the ethnomethodological approach provides they argue that cultural ethnography has become a vehicle for "producing social and cultural texts." Instead of acting on behalf of the members, the researchers have become wordsmiths plying their theories and understandings of culture.

Simply put, what is behind the ethnomethodologist's fear is that the new ethnographies are not kosher. However, the uproar following the publication of Crabtree at al.'s "ethnography considered harmful" paper suggests otherwise. Just as cognitive ethnography has provided new insights and ways of thinking about work practice, user experience and technology design so, too, are culturally-inspired ethnographies providing fresh insights into the everyday practices and appropriation of a diversity of technologies. The debate over what is acceptable HCI practice has long passed and more constructive debate about what contributions the different kinds of ethnography have to offer is to be welcomed.

Theory-driven Ethnography in a Nutshell

As discussed above, Rogers (1997) noted how drawing implications for design both belittles the ethnographer's rich descriptive accounts while appearing tokenistic to the designers. Moreover, it is often ill-suited to the kinds of generalizations that are expected and readily made from the findings of other kinds of user studies and conceptual analyses in HCI. More recently, (Dourish, 2006, 2007) extended this argument, critiquing the "implications for design" further. He stresses how the expectation that has arisen in HCI — that ethnographic field studies need to enumerate specific "implications for design" in order to be relevant to HCI is misplaced. Instead of assuming a researcher can "go out and find facts lying around in the world, dust them off, and bring them home to inform, educate, and delight" he argues that ethnography is deeply relevant for design, but that its value is elsewhere. This can get lost, when only focusing on the value of the design implications presented (or not) at the end of a field study. "Such lists underplay the more radical implications that may be caught up in ethnographic work; indeed, if the ethnographer returns from the field with little more than the lesson that the object in question should be green, should fit in a handbag, and should run for at least three weeks on two AA batteries, then I might venture that there isn't much to the ethnography." (Dourish, 2007, p5).

Importantly, the *theoretical* work of ethnography needs to be brought out much more, given its interpretive, analytic practice (Dourish, 2007). Moreover, the practice of reading for theory needs to be more up front since it may prove to be where the really significant "implications" are. This can involve examining ethnographical materials of cultural practices and the anthropologist's theoretical interpretations of them, which may be produced outside of the domain of technology development. The detailed and rich accounts of human experience can be read outside the terms of the specific field study, and, arguably provide guidance that is generalizable to other contexts — something that the ethnomethodologists have struggled with because of their adherence to the specific details. It does, however, require that the HCI researcher immerse themselves in the thick of cultural anthropology, which for some may be a joy, while for others too much of a journey into the unknown. For those with the time and curiosity, it can open up new possibilities for thinking about the design space, user experience and technologies.

What impact have ethnomethodology and ethnography had on HCI?

Ethnomethodology and ethnographic approaches have had a big impact on HCI and CSCW, by providing many insightful detailed descriptions of work and everyday practices. While the locus of their value has been contested, in terms of whether they should be making a theoretical or empirical contribution, they continue to be considered a fundamental part of doing user studies. They have informed design in various ways; suggesting new prototypes, new work practices and the conduct of user's interactions with technologies, in terms of how best they can be accomplished, by following the way they are conducted in human-human interactions and actions. Less successful, have been attempts to enrich design discourse, through providing a new lingua franca of concepts.

5.6   CSCW THEORIES

The field of CSCW emerged in the late 1980s, when a critical mass of researchers proposed an agenda for the social and organizational aspects of computing. The framing was concerned primarily with how computer technologies could be designed to support collaborative working practices. A particular interest was on how computer support could be developed to ameliorate the negative aspects of group working while enhancing or extending the positive aspects.

Unlike HCI, where cognitive psychology was largely the dominant theory that helped shape the field, initially a number of disparate theories were drawn upon from the social sciences, including organization, sociological and social psychology. They were primarily concerned with how organizations, groups and teams work together, but were approached from different levels and granularity of analysis, methodological stances and epistemologies. For example, theories arising from sociology included Gerson and Star's (1986) articulation work together with approaches stemming from Marxism, such as the division of labor, that adopted a critical stance towards how work is accomplished; theories coming from organizational psychology, included sociotechnical systems, with a focus on job satisfaction and work design principles, such as Enid Mumford's classic ETHICs (effective technical and human implementation of computer systems) method (see Mumford and Weir, 1979; and from social psychology, a number of group theories about social phenomena were cherry picked, such as why groups exert less effort than individuals (see McGrath, 1984).

A perusal of the early CSCW literature suggests that many more theories were brought in from a variety of perspectives, as CSCW established itself, compared with how HCI evolved. Part of the reason for this is that the study of the social covers a much broader range of interactions, concerns and topics — from why people behave differently in groups than by themselves to how organizations manage their businesses, and hence there were more disciplines and theories to draw upon by the diversity of researchers attracted to the emerging field. Arguably, this denser level of theorizing resulted in a wider range of applications and systems being analyzed, informed and generated (e.g., decision-making systems, workflow systems, computer-mediated communication, social networking).

It is simply not possible to do justice to all the theoretical developments in CSCW in one small section. Instead, I mention a few of them here to give a flavor of the different kinds that came to the fore and the ways they were applied. There are, of course, parallels with HCI theory development, in terms of how researchers saw their role in helping to account for, generate hypotheses, analyze and inform the design of user studies and computing systems. However, there are some differences, notably, in the scale and scope of the theories that address the complexity and uncertainty of how organizations and groups work, compared to the early attempts at predictability and controllability of individual cognition/user interaction.

Group theories were able to provide insights about social behavior and directions for how technologies might support their work activities more effectively. A classic was McGrath's (1991) theory and typology of group modes, known as TIP, that was influential in shifting from lab-based studies of groups to considering how they operate in real world settings (Grudin, 2008). He argued that groups engage in four essential modes of operation (inception, problem-solving, conflict resolution, and execution) for which there are three functions for each of these (production, group well-being and member support). Grudin (2008) notes how taking these all into account and their interdependencies results in a quite different way of viewing technology design and adoption; one that avoids the pitfalls of focusing exclusively on performance or productivity, which in, themselves, are likely to fail because of all the things that happen in groups, as identified by McGrath's typology.

Despite there being a large body of social psychology theories about small group behaviors, only a few were brought to the attention of researchers in CSCW (Kraut, 2003). The most well known was social loafing (individuals don't work as hard as when they work by themselves as they think the outcome of their efforts are being combined with those of others). Kraut (2003) has written extensively how these can be systematically applied to the design of group support systems, such as brainstorming tools and group decision-support tools. They have also been used to explain why groups behave differently or unexpectedly when participating in online groups and communities. An example he uses is the phenomenon of lurking or non-contribution in online communities, where people join an online community or other discussion group but only take on a passive role, reading what others had written and not contributing ideas or comments, themselves. Kraut (2003) suggests that as well as couching CSCW behaviors in these identified phenomena, *general* guidelines that have been derived from the theories in social psychology, such as social loafing (e.g., Karau and Williams, 1993), could be turned into *design* guidelines to suggest how to deal with them, by setting up technology in certain ways that would encourage or constrain more equal participation. In doing so, he shows how other factors and theories can be considered when trying to increase group participation levels to be more even, such as making the group appear attractive (using principles and theories of interpersonal attraction).

A controversial use of language theory

Theories of how people act through language, notably speech act theory, were used to develop the language/action framework, which in turn, was used to inform the design of a system, called the Coordinator, to help people work more effectively by improving the way they communicate with one another (Winograd and Flores, 1986). Speech act theory explains the functions utterances have in conversations (Austin, 1962; Searle, 1969). They can be direct (e.g., "I hereby declare you man and wife") or indirect (when someone says "It's hot in here" what they really mean is it OK to open the window). The Coordinator was designed to enable emails to be sent between people in the form of explicit speech acts. When sending someone a request, say "Could you get the report to me," the sender was also required to select the menu option "request." This was placed in the subject header of the message, thereby explicitly specifying the nature of the speech act. Thus, the Coordinator was designed to provide a straight forward conversational structure, allowing users to make clear the status of their work and, likewise, to be clear about the status of others' work in terms of various commitments.

The application of speech act theory in this manner, however, was subject to much criticism at the time by others in the research community who were incensed by the assumptions that speech act theory could be usefully applied to the design of a work system. Many heated debates ensued, often politically charged. A major concern was the extent to which the system *prescribed* how people should communicate. It was pointed out that asking users to specify *explicitly* the nature of their implicit speech acts was contrary to what they normally do in conversations. Moreover, forcing people to communicate in such an artificial way was regarded as highly undesirable. While some people may be very blatant about what they want doing, when they want it done by, and what they are prepared to do, most people tend to use more subtle and indirect forms of communication to advance their collaborations with others. The problem that Winograd and Flores came up against was people's resistance to radically change their way of communicating. Indeed, many of the people who tried using the Coordinator System in their work organizations either abandoned it or resorted to using only the free-form message facility, which had no explicit demands associated with it. It was asking too much of them to change the way they communicated and worked. However, it was successful in other kinds of organizations, namely those that are highly structured and need a highly structured system to support them. In particular, it has been much more successful in organizations, such as large manufacturing divisions of companies, where there is a great need for management of orders and where previous support has been mainly in the form of paper forms and inflexible task-specific data processing applications (Winograd, 1994).

Coordination theories were also influential, explaining the coordination work that is needed to enable groups to synchronize their efforts as a concerted action (e.g., Malone and Crowston, 1990). In an extensive review of his and others' work in this area, Schmidt (2011) expounded the coordination mechanisms that are integral to cooperative work, including the role played by constructs such as checklists, plans, blueprints, and operating procedures. Drawing from Marxism and other praxis-based theories, he established how material artifacts and practices are constructed, appropriated, applied and adapted, providing a theoretical basis from which to analyze coordination practices when new cooperative systems are being proposed or introduced into an organization.

Other theories that have been taken from critical sociology and the social sciences and shown how they can be applied in CSCW include actor network theory (see Latour, 2005; Law, 1987) and semiotic theory (De Souza, 2005). The former was developed as a reaction to the vague all encompassing terms prominent in sociology at the time, such as institutions, organizations, states and nations, replacing them with a more realistic and smaller set of associations for describing the very nature of societies, that encompasses both human individual actors and non-human, non individual entities. The latter draws on concepts from semiotics and computer science to investigate the relationship between designers and users, who are viewed as interlocutors in a communication process that takes place through the interface of words, graphics, and behavior.

5.7   ACTIVITY THEORY

Activity Theory (AT) is a product of Soviet Psychology that explained human behavior in terms of our practical activity with the world. It originated as part of the attempt to produce a Marxist Psychology, an enterprise usually associated with Vygotsky (e.g., 1962) and later Leontiev (e.g., 1978, 1989). In the last 30 years, versions of AT have become popular elsewhere, particularly in Scandinavia, Germany and now in the U.S. and UK. The newer "versions" of AT have been popular in research investigating "applied" problems, particularly those to do with work, technology and education.

Its conceptual framework was assumed to have much to offer to HCI, in terms of providing a means of analyzing actions and interactions with artifacts within a historical and cultural context (Bannon and Bødker, 1991; Bødker, 1989; Kuutti, 1996; Nardi, 1996). It first appeared in HCI in the late 1980s when Susanne Bødker (1989) applied it to the design of user interfaces for newspaper production. It was then brought to mainstream attention through her collaboration with Liam Bannon (Bannon and Bødker, 1991) where they showed how it could be used to analyze actions and interactions with artifacts within historical and cultural contexts. They argued that this kind of conceptual analysis could be used to inform the design of technologies that better suited workers in their work environments. Since their pioneering work, numerous edited volumes, case studies, PhD dissertations, and special journal issues have been published showing how AT can be adapted and applied to a diversity of areas, particularly the analysis of work, technology and education.

Besides Bødker and Bannon's seminal work, a number of researchers have promulgated its merits and value for HCI, notably, Yjro Engestrøm, Kari Kuutti, Olav Bertelsen, Wendy MacKay, David Redmiles and Jakob Bardram. But perhaps the most ardent and longstanding proponents are Bonnie Nardi and Victor Kaptelinin. Since the mid 1990s, they have tirelessly promoted the AT approach, arguing that it has much to offer HCI researchers and practitioners, especially compared with other cognitive and social approaches that have been imported into the field (Nardi and Kaptelinin, 2012). They claim it provides "the rigor and dedication of the scientific method of traditional cognitive science with the much needed attention to social and contextual factors necessary to HCI studies" (Kaptelinin and Nardi, 1997). Part of their mission has been to provide a broad framework for describing the structure, development and context of computer-supported activities that is easily usable by practitioners. This has included giving tutorials, workshops and an Activity checklist for identifying the most important factors influencing the use of computer technologies in a particular setting (Kaptelinin et al., 1999). Besides Nardi and Kaptelinin's reworking of AT for an HCI audience, several of the other AT researchers have elaborated and adapted Leontiev's (1978) original framework with applied goals in mind. Notable, is the highly cited work of Kuutti's (1996) extension of the hierarchical framework to show how information technology can be used to support different kinds of activities at different levels, and Nardi's (1996) adapted framework showing how it can be of value for examining data and eliciting new sets of design concerns. Nardi recast data from a field study that she had carried out earlier to compare the benefits of task-specific versus generic application software for making slides (Nardi and Johnson, 1994). In doing this exercise second time round, but with the added benefit of the conceptual framework of activity theory at hand, she found she was able to make more sense of her data. In particular, she cites how it enabled her to ask a more appropriate set of questions that allowed her subsequently to come up with an alternative set of recommendations about software architectures for the application of slide-making.

Activity Theory in a Nutshell

Activity Theory explains cultural practices (e.g., work, school) in the developmental, cultural and historical context in which they occur, by describing them in terms of "activities." The backbone of the theory is presented as a hierarchical model of activity that frames consciousness at different levels. These are operations, actions and activities. A number of principles are also proposed.

Focusing the analysis around the concept of an activity can help to identify tensions between the different elements of the system. An example of where it was used to show these was MacKay et al.'s (2000) study of users working with a new software tool that identified 19 shifts in attention between different parts of the tool interface and the task at hand. Some users spent so much time engaged in these shifts that they lost track of their original task. Using the theory helped the evaluators to focus on relevant incidents.

There are two key models: (i) an activity model and (ii) the mediating role of artifacts.

(i) The "classic" individual model (Figure 5.1)

At the bottom level of the model are operations, routinized behaviors that require little conscious attention, e.g., rapid typing. At an intermediate level are actions that are characterized by conscious planning, e.g., producing an index. The top level is the activity, and that provides a minimum meaningful context for understanding the individual actions, e.g., writing a chapter. There may be many different operations capable of fulfilling an action, and many actions capable of serving the same activity.

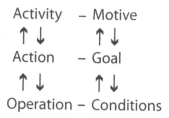

Figure 5.1: The original activity theory model.

Activities can be identified on the basis of the motives that elicit them, actions on the basis of conscious goals that guide them, and operations by the conditions necessary to attain the goals. However, there is an intimate and fluid link between levels. Actions can become operations as they become more automatic and operations can become actions when an operation encounters an obstacle, thus requiring conscious planning. Similarly, there is no strict demarcation between action and activity. If the motive changes then an activity can become an action. It is also important to realize that activities are not self-contained. Activities relate to others while actions may be part of different activities, and so on.

(ii) Mediating role of Artifacts

Artifacts can be physical, such as a book or a stone, or they can be abstract, such as a system of symbols or a set of rules. Physical artifacts have physical properties that cause humans to respond to them as direct objects to be acted upon. They also embody a set of social practices, their design reflecting a history of particular use. Leontiev (1981) describes the process of learning what these inherent properties are as one of appropriation, signifying the active nature of the learning that is needed. The kind of learning involved is one of identifying and participating in the activity appropriate to the artifact.

Consider an infant learning to feed with a spoon. Leontiev (1981) observes that, at first, the infant carries the spoon to its mouth as though it were handling any other object, not considering the need to hold it horizontal. Over time, with adult guidance, the spoon is shaped in the way it is because of the social practice — the activity — of feeding and, in turn, the infant's task is to learn that relationship — to discover what practice(s) the object embodies. By contrast a spoon dropped into the cage of a mouse, say, will only ever have the status of just another physical object — no different from that of a stone.

The idea of abstract artifacts follows from the idea of mediation, i.e., a fundamental characteristic of human development is the change from a direct mode of acting on the world to one that is mediated by something else. In AT, the artifacts involved in an activity mediate between the elements of it. The social context of an activity is also considered central. Even when seemingly working alone, an individual is still engaged in activities that are given meaning by a wider set of practices.

Engeström's (1990) extension of Activity Theory, known as "developmental work research" has also been influential in CSCW. His framework was designed to include other concepts (e.g., contradictions, community, rules and division of labor) that were pertinent to work contexts and which could provide conceptual leverage for exploring these. He widened the focus from the individual triangle of a single activity (subject, activity, and object) to include supra-individual concepts — tools, rules, community, and division of labor. By tools is meant the artifacts, signs, and means that mediate the subject and object; by community is meant those who share the same object; by rules is meant a set of agreed conventions and policies covering what it means to be a member of that community (set by laws, parents, managers, boards, etc.); and by division of labor is meant the primary means of classifying the labor in a workplace, e.g., manager, engineer, receptionist.

The extended versions allow consideration of networks of interrelated activities — forming an activity system. It has been used to analyze a range of work settings — usually where there is a problem with existing or newly implemented technology — providing both macro and micro level accounts. Several others have adopted Engeström's approach and have used the model to identify a range of problems and tensions in various settings. Some have taken this variant and adapted it further to suit their needs. These include Halloran et al.'s (2002) Activity Space framework for analyzing collaborative learning, Spasser's (2002) "realist" approach for analyzing the design and use of digital libraries and Collins et al.'s (2002) model employed to help identify user requirements for customer support engineers. One of the putative benefits from having a more extensive framework with a set of conceptual foci is how they structure and scaffold the researcher/designer in their analysis:

"We found that activity system tensions provide rich insights into system dynamics and opportunities for the evolution of the system." (Collins et al. op cit, p58).

The extended analytic frameworks have proven attractive because they offer a "rhetorical force of naming" (Halverson, 2002, p247), providing a set of terms that the analyst can use to match to instances in their data and, in so doing, systematically identify problems. However, it still relies largely on the analyst's interpretative skills and orientation as to what course to take through the data and how to relate this to which concepts of the framework. In some ways this is redolent of the problem discussed earlier concerning the application of cognitive modeling approaches to real world problems. There is little guidance (since it essentially is a subjective judgment) to determine the different kinds of activities — a lot depends on understanding the context in which they occur.

It is argued, therefore, that to achieve a level of competence in understanding and applying the various AT frameworks still requires considerable learning and experience (Rogers, 2008b). Hence, while, variants of the activity system model can be applied more readily, they are most useful for those who have developed them and understand activity theory in its historic context. When given to others not familiar with the original theory, their utility is arguably less and can even be problematic. For example, the basic abstractions of the model, like object and subject, were found to be difficult to follow, and easily confused with everyday uses of the terms when used by design and engineering teams (who were initially unfamiliar with them) to discuss user requirements (Collins et al., 2002).

AT does not provide a clear methodological prescription for the description or analysis of behavior as a set of procedures to be followed. Identifying elements in the framework is highly dependent on individual interpretation. One of the biggest problems with doing an AT analysis is working out when something should be described as a top-level activity and when something is better described as a lower-level action. For example, completing a software project is considered to be a top-level activity, while programming a module as an action. However, equally, programming a module could be viewed as an activity — if that was the object of the subject (person).

González (2006) tried to overcome this problem of distinguishing between levels by introducing a new intermediate concept to sit between an action and an activity and which describes "how tasks are aggregated and thematically connected on higher level units of work" (p53). He called this new level as one of engagements, which "thematically connect chains of actions towards the achievement of a purpose" (p9). Five types of engagements were outlined as specific units of work: requests, projects, problems, events and recurrents (p156). His idea behind analyzing actions/activities as types of work practices — rather than trying to decide whether to label them as actions or activities — is appealing since it can reveal more about what actually happens in the workplace. As part of the extended form of analysis, he suggested that the various actions that take place be viewed in relation to their higher-level purpose, such as a group manager composing an email and then sending it out to his team to motivate them. The emphasis is also on the way actions relate to other actions, rather than on how actions are performed through operations. The role of communication is also stressed in terms of how workers justify their motives and choice of which action/activity to follow at a given time.

Potentially, the outcome of performing this additional level of analysis is a richer interpretation of the field study data, and arguably a better understanding of how work gets accomplished on a moment-to-moment, what-to-do-next basis within the wider context of the purpose of the work. It switches the focus of the analysis from agonizing about the level at which to label something to examining the types of working spheres/engagements people have and pursue in terms of their temporal patterns, priorities and interdependencies with the work of others. It also enables a better linkage between the detailed ethnographic data collected in field studies and the conceptual labels of the framework.

What impact has Activity Theory had in HCI?

AT has been very popular, especially among Ph.D. students, as an explanatory framework. It has been used to couch and ground qualitative data in a variety of contexts. Numerous tensions and contradictions have been identified in workplace settings leading to the identification of specific needs for new technological tools. Its value has been in providing a structured framework that breaks down into a set of conceptual tools that can then be mapped onto features of complex, real-world contexts. In so doing, problems and opportunities for new interventions can be elicited. It has been popularized in Scandinavia, UK and the U.S.

5.8   GROUNDED THEORY

Grounded theory is not a theory *per se* but an approach that aims to help researchers develop theory from the systematic analysis and interpretation of empirical data, i.e., the theory derived is grounded in the data. Similar to AT, it has been a very popular choice amongst researchers wanting to make sense of the qualitative data they have collected, such as ethnographic video. The approach was originally developed by Glaser and Strauss (1967) and has been adopted and adapted by several researchers for different situations. Glaser and Strauss also individually (and with others) developed the theory in slightly different ways. Glaser (1992) documented the way the variants differ.

Grounded Theory in a Nutshell

The aim of grounded theory is to develop a theory that fits a set of collected data. In a nutshell, it is "a set of well-developed concepts related through statements of relationship, which together constitute an integrated framework that can be used to explain or predict phenomena" (Strauss and Corbin, 1998). To develop a "grounded" theory requires the researcher iteratively switching between data collection and data analysis. Initially, data is collected and analyzed to identify categories, then that analysis leads to the need for further data collection, which is analyzed, and more data is collected. Hence, data gathering is driven by the emerging theory and finishes when no further insights are gained from the alternating.

The goal of the grounded theory approach is to identify and define the properties and dimensions of relevant categories and then to use these as the basis for constructing a theory. There are essentially three kinds of coding:

(i) *Open coding* where categories, their properties, and dimensions are discovered in the data.

(ii) *Axial coding* where the categories are systematically fleshed out and related to their subcategories.

(iii) *Selective coding* where categories are refined and integrated to form a larger theoretical scheme.

Strauss and Corbin (1998) suggest collecting data that includes written records of analysis and diagrammatic representations of categories (which they call memos and diagrams). To help identify and characterize relevant categories, the researcher is encouraged to:

- question the data in order to generate ideas or consider different ways of looking at the data.

- analyze a word, phrase, or sentence, in order to understand better the meaning of an utterance, which in turn can trigger different ways of viewing the data.

- analyze the data through comparing objects or between abstract categories.

    Charmaz (2011) provides a practical guide in detail of the steps involved in coding.

In contrast to AT, there isn't a set of concepts or framework that can be used to make sense of the data. Instead, researchers need to draw on their own theoretical backgrounds. For example, when Sarker et al. (2001) used the grounded theory approach to develop a model of collaboration in virtual teams they drew from their background in the social sciences, using ideas from human conduct and social structure. Furniss et al. (2011) have used theoretical ideas from both distributed cognition and resilience engineering (a new way of thinking about safety, that enables organizations to create processes that are robust and flexible and which use resources proactively in the face of disruptions or ongoing production and economic pressures).

The types of questions researchers pose and iterate is key to which kinds of concepts they end up eliciting. Dourish et al. (2004a) used semi-structured interviews and grounded theory to examine how people answer the question "Is this system secure enough for what I want to do now?," in the context of ubiquitous and mobile technologies. This qualitative approach was used to explore the issues before moving on to develop more detailed questions, but their conclusions included suggested design modifications to take this perspective on security into account. Grinter (1998) carried out interviewing and observation at a number of sites as part of her qualitative approach to gathering data and developing a grounded theory about recomposition in software companies. She also engaged in participant observation, by helping to conduct usability studies, reviewing system architectures, facilitating project retrospectives, and process design.

Much depends on the skills of the analyst and their background, in knowing how to process the data using the layered coding scheme. It is also very time-consuming. Charmaz (2011) also emphasizes that, as the name suggests, developing theory is central to using Grounded Theory. Importantly, it provides a method for researchers to develop theory rather than apply existing theory. Its value for HCI lies in how a researcher can skillfully iterate between data collection and analysis to create a new theoretical understanding. This does not have to be a totally new theory replete with concepts and relations; but can comprise a frame work that demonstrates a hierarchy of classes and sub-classes for a given setting for which data has been collected.

What impact has the grounded theory approach had in HCI?

Grounded Theory has been used widely in HCI, providing insights into people's values, understanding and experience with technology (Furniss et al., 2011). It has become increasingly popular in interaction design to answer specific questions and design concerns (Grinter, 2011). It provides a method for generating new theory, by iterating between data collection and coding. This differs from other top-down approaches, which provide a theoretical framework to match instances or patterns found in the collected data against an existing set of concepts.

5.9 HYBRID THEORIES

To conclude this section, I briefly touch upon some of the attempts in HCI to synthesize a diversity of concepts from different theories and disciplines. The rationale for the over arching approaches was to provide more extensive and if possible, unified theories, compared with importing concepts arising from only one discipline. The late Leight Star (1996), for example, was very skilful at bringing together different strands of disparate theories to provide fresh insights. In one instance, she looked at similarities between Activity Theory and symbolic interactionalism (originating from American pragmatism) that showed links between them.

Pirolli and Card's (1997) information foraging food-theory (IFT) was also very insightful and provided a completely new way of thinking about searching on the web. In particular, it opened up the field of information visualization to many more researchers, leading to the development of new kinds of graphical representations and browsing tools. They describe searching for and making sense of information in terms of a number of concepts borrowed from evolution, biology and anthropology and classical information processing theory: "in many ways analogous to evolutionary ecological explanations of food-foraging strategies in anthropology and behavior ecology" (p5). The search strategies are viewed in terms of making correct decision points, which are influenced by the presence or absence of "scent." If the scent is strong enough, the person will make the correct choices; if not they will follow a more random walk.

The most overarching theories of HCI attempted to integrate theories from different fields at multiple levels of analysis. An ambitious example was Mantovani's (1996) eclectic model of HCI, that combined a diverse range of concepts and research findings from computer-supported cooperative work (CSCW), computer-mediated communication (CMC) and distributed artificial intelligence (DAI). The outcome was a three-level conceptual model of social context that combined top-down with bottom-up approaches in order to analyze social norms and activities. Barnard et al.'s (2000) "Systems of Interactors" theoretical frame work also drew upon several overlapping layers of macro theory and micro theory. Which level of theory is relevant depends on the nature of the problem being investigated.

While providing more comprehensive theories of HCI, these kinds of unified frameworks have proven difficult for other researchers to use in practice. It is much more unwieldy to juggle with multiple concepts, constraints and levels when analyzing a problem space and/or designing a system, compared with using a constrained framework that has far fewer interlinked concepts. While being attractive theories, it turns out that it is largely the authors, themselves, that have used them. Another case, perhaps, of the toothbrush syndrome.

CHAPTER 6

Contemporary Theory

A distinguishing feature of Contemporary art that set it apart from Modernism was that much of the work was considered socially conscious, being interpreted and construed from cultural perspectives, such as feminism, multiculturalism and globalization. A wide range of ideals, methods and practices were promoted, explored and pursued, incorporating a number of philosophical and critical methods that collectively became coined as "postmodernist." A "theory industry" was born (Stiles, 1996) where many new modes of theoretical debate and scholarly discourse took shape. Critical theory, in its various manifestations, took center stage, questioning the status of texts and the role of the authors who speak through them.

There are similar parallels that took place between the shift from modern to contemporary HCI, with the emergence of a more self-conscious reflexivity and social conscience, as exemplified by the third paradigm (Harrison et al., 2007). Different human values came to the forefront, extending and superseding previously mainstream HCI goals to improve efficiency and productivity. Cultural perspectives, such as feminism, multiculturalism and critical theory, were also promoted.

6.1 HUMAN VALUES

Contemporary HCI theory began in the mid to late 2000s. Debates surfaced about what HCI researchers do, what practitioners should be doing, whether they should be doing it and what their respective social responsibilities ought to be in a changing world of increasing technology use and dependency (see Blythe et al., 2008; Dourish et al., 2004b). The manifesto "Being Human: Human-Computer Interaction in the Year 2020" paved the way for a different kind of value-driven agenda. Concerns were voiced that if HCI was to continue to be of relevance in the 21st Century, it needed to change tack (Harper et al., 2008). New directions proposed included operationalizing contemporary society's aspirations and desires for self-understanding and expression. But to do so, needed a different set of conceptual tools that could tackle the empirical, philosophical and moral investigation of technology.

Given the pace at which HCI has moved forwards in its short history (Grudin, 2012), and its propensity to join forces with other disciplines, it seems well positioned to take on this new set of social, moral and cultural challenges. Not being strongly wedded to a particular set of techniques or paradigms that are steeped in tradition, means it can rapidly change course, abandon "old" ways of studying and embrace the new.

Indeed, a new set of concepts, tools and methods is beginning to appear that are intended to address the wider range of human values, rather than well versed human needs (e.g., computers should be easy to learn, easy to use, etc.). They include getting to grips with *life* goals (cf. to *user's* goals), such as how people can pursue healthier, more meaningful and enjoyable lifestyles; and probing technology's underbelly as it becomes more insidious; including looking at how governments and organizations have become more reliant on computer technology to control society while individuals have started to use it in more criminal ways, making people worry more about what information is tracked, analyzed and stored about them.

Action Research is one such socially responsible approach that is being promoted in HCI. It provides methods and approaches for conducting democratic and collaborative research with members of a community (Hayes, 2011). In particular, it offers theoretical lenses, methodological approaches, and pragmatic guidance for conducting socially relevant, collaborative and engaged research (Stringer, 2007). Where it differs from previous participatory design approaches, is that while primarily seeking to help with practical concerns, it also aspires to scientific rigor and the promotion of sustainable social change. To achieve these three goals, a cyclical methodology is followed, with an emphasis on problem formulation, intervention design, deployment (i.e., "action"), observation of the effects of the action, reflection and then redefinition of the problem. A further distinction is to come up with a solution that improves on previous ones and which helps all those engaged in the project learn through the actions they take.

Being engaged in socially aware and responsible research involves asking different questions, such as what are culturally appropriate technologies for the home (Bell et al., 2003). A range of contemporary topics have begun to be explored with quite different questions being asked than previous usability or hedonistic ones, including health and well-being, climate change, feminism, multiculturalism, globalization, world peace and poverty (Shneiderman, 2011).

Adding Understanding to the Mix

As part of the new agenda for HCI, the *Being Human* report (Harper et al., 2008) proposed extending the canonical 4-stage iterative model of user-centered design by adding another stage. The new stage, called *understand,* is intended to address explicitly the human values that the technology in question will be designed to serve. Depending on the values of interest, the understand stage can draw on disciplines as diverse as philosophy, psychology, art, sociology, cultural studies, and architecture. These investigations are intended to point to fundamental research that needs to be conducted, relevant research that has already been carried out, or some combination of the two.

Some researchers have gone far afield, decamping to developing countries in an effort to use and develop ICT to help reduce poverty, starvation, improve sanitation, etc. Many of these new IT projects are well intentioned. However, concerns within the HCI community have started to be

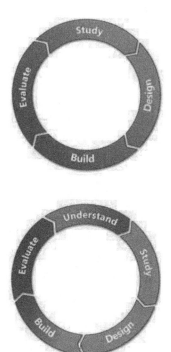

Figure 6.1: The conventional user-centered research and design process (top) and the extended five-stage research and design process (bottom) encompassing a new stage of conceptual analysis or "understanding" of human values. (From Harper et al., 2008.)

voiced about the motivations for looking "out there" (Taylor, 2011). In particular, there is a sense of unease for those who waver between wanting to make the world a better place while needing to collect ethnographic materials to publish and furnish theory building. Is it possible to do both and is it desirable? The dilemma of trying to be a participant and a researcher has ramifications for the balance of research and development. Here, I just give a flavor of the new theoretical approaches that have been selected, imported and developed within Contemporary HCI. But, it is acknowledged that many of the new theories should be viewed in the wider context of the researcher's social responsibility — and in the fullness of time it will be interesting to see how the moral narrative evolves for areas such as ICTD, HCI for peace and animal-computer interaction (Mancini, 2011).

I have chosen to select four major "turns" to characterize and distinguish between the main kinds of HCI contemporary theory. These are:

(a) turn to design

(b) turn to culture

(c) turn to the wild

(d) turn to embodiment

The rhetorical device of "a turn" has become popularized as a way of noting a change in the framing of HCI ever since the phrase "turn to the social" was coined in the 1990s. It is acknowledged there are several other turns that have appeared in the HCI literature, besides the ones listed above, such as those about particular topics or areas, such as emotion, enjoyment and sustainability, and a turn to "practice." For the purpose of this chapter, however, the turns to design, culture, the wild and embodiment are only covered.

6.2   TURN TO DESIGN

Since the early 1990s, design has been considered central to HCI, beginning with a focus on software design, user-centered design and interface design (e.g., Karat , 1991; Winograd, 1996). How to gather user requirements and developing methods that could better inform user-centered design have been two central themes. Case studies, such as the Mac interface and VisiCalc, were drawn upon to illustrate good practice in software design.

The turn to design as a more theoretical concern began in earnest during the 2000s when researchers began discussing how design theory and critical design could play a more central role in HCI. Winograd's early paper (1997) proposing that interaction design was about the "interspaces" inhabited by "multiple people, workstations, servers and other devices" in a complex web of inter-actions, led others to consider how to create design spaces within which people could communicate through. Shön's (1987) influential ideas on reflective practice were also brought into the mix.

A landmark book by Löwgren and Stolterman (2004) called *Thoughtful Interaction Design* drew from a range of Art, Design and Humanities theories, including English Literature. A running theme throughout was *not* about how to do interaction design but how to *think* about it. This shift from prescription to reflection drew attention to the complexity of design. Reducing it to a recipe book of steps to be followed or lessons learned was considered an over-simplification. Instead, much interpretation and understanding is needed of the choices that have to be made throughout the design process, often between trade-offs. This is where design theory can inspire; liberating "the designer from preconceived notions and conceptions of how the design process can be performed" and using it to "create new conditions for design, different patterns of thinking and acting, new design principles, and a general understanding of the conditions for creative and innovative work" (p8).

The idea that interaction design be informed by theories from aesthetics, ethics, politics and ideology was a radical departure for many in software design. Instead of thinking in terms of which methods to use *per se*, another push was towards thinking about how to use them *responsibly*, by applying them sensitively, skillfully and appropriately. Concepts such as pleasure, user experi-ence, enjoyment and play provided much new food for thought, enabling designers to contemplate what it means to design for lifestyles — and as something we *live with*, not simply something we *use* (Hallnäs and Redström, 2002).

More recently, there has been a move towards accountability: it has been increasingly argued that designers have a responsibility towards what they choose to examine, analyze and design for. Debates about what this might entail have been aired; new terms have surfaced, such as design activism (Light, 2009), sustainable design (Blevis, 2007), inclusive design (Vanderheiden, 2008), value-sensitive design (Friedman et al., 2006) and worth-sensitive design (Cockton, 2006).

As part of the trend towards more critical reflection, researchers have also looked to various forms of philosophy that they see as providing deeper ways of understanding technology-mediated experience. For example, Fallman (2011) has presented the philosophies of technology by Borgmann (1992) and Ihde (1993) to the HCI community as a way of helping them articulate the range of human values in relation to technology: introducing notions of *device paradigm* and *non-neutrality of technology mediated experience*, respectively, while Cockton (2010) has introduced Badiou's (1988) theory on *design situations* that in itself, was a response to postmodernist ontologies. These kinds of philosophical theories provide epistemologies about the state of the world and what constitutes reality. For those with a proclivity for, or background in, this kind of philosophy, they can provide alternative ways of reading and understanding the ethics of technology and the value-based choices designers make and connecting between them. For others, they can appear somewhat overwhelming.

A more accessible approach to philosophizing about HCI was McCarthy and Wright's (2004) *Technology as Experience* framework, where the *phenomenology* of the user experience was discussed and applied to design practice. A particular focus was the *felt experience*, i.e., how something is felt by the user. The ideas were drawn from Pragmatism, and in particular, the philosophical writings of Dewey that emphasize the sense-making aspects of human experiences. This understanding is applied to the whole experience of a technology that people have in terms of their interconnected aspects, rather than as fragmented aspects (e.g., its usability or utility). But defining a felt experience is very difficult because it is nebulous and ever-present to us, just as swimming in water is to a fish. Their way of tackling this was to describe it in holistic and metaphorical terms.

Technology as Experience in a Nutshell

McCarthy and Wright (2004) propose four core threads that make up our holistic experiences: compositional, sensual, emotional and spatio-temporal. The sensual thread is concerned with our sensory engagement with a situation, and can be equated with the level of absorption people have with various technological devices and applications, most notable being computer games, cell phones and chatrooms, where users can be highly absorbed in their interactions at a sensory level. The emotional thread includes emotions such as sorrow, anger, joy and happiness. Emotions are intertwined with the situation in which they arise, e.g., a person becomes angry with a computer because it does not work properly. Emotions also involve making judgments of value. For example, when purchasing a new cell phone, people may be drawn to the ones that are most cool-looking but be in an emotional turmoil because they are the most expensive. The compositional thread is concerned with the narrative part of an experience, as it unfolds, and the way a person makes sense of them. For example, when shopping online, the choices laid out to people can lead them in a coherent way to making a desired purchase or they can lead to frustrating experiences resulting in no purchase being made. When in this situation, people ask themselves questions such as "What is this about? Where am I? What has happened? What is going to happen next? What would happen if …?" The spatio-temporal thread refers to the space and time in which our experiences take place and their effect upon those experiences, including how we talk of time speeding up, standing still and slowing down, and needing one's own space.

The threads are meant as ideas to help designers think and talk more clearly and concretely about the relationship between technology and experience. For example, when buying clothes online, the framework can be used to capture the whole gamut of experiences, including: the fear or joy of needing to buy a new outfit; the time and place where it can be purchased, e.g., online stores or shopping mall; the tensions of how to engage with the vendor, e.g., the pushy sales assistant or an anonymous website; the value judgment involved in contemplating the cost and how much one is prepared to spend; the internal monologue that goes on where questions are asked such as will it look good on me, what size should I buy, do I have shoes to match, do I need to try it on, how easy will it be to wash, will I need to iron it each time and how often will I be able to wear it. All of these aspects can be described in terms of the four threads and in so doing highlight which aspects are more important for a given product. Such interlinked facets and concerns are what most of us engage with in our everyday actions and interactions with others.

The threads may provide metaphors for thinking about design, but how well do they inform design in practice? Heather Collins and Aaron Loehrlein (id-book.com) describe in a case study how they used them as inputs for web design. They found the threads to be helpful in thinking about the balance of the different experiences they were hoping to elicit. Since Wright and McCarthy (2010) developed their ideas further, explicating what is meant by *experience-centered design* from a humanistic approach when designing digital technologies.

Besides social responsibility, other design values that have been promoted are ludic and playful ones that promote curiosity, exploration and aesthetic enjoyment amongst people when they encounter new technologies. The idea is to trigger more reflection in users/people on what they notice and how it changes their perspective of and relation to the environment. A diversity of artifacts has been created within a playful context, including a periscope (Rogers et al., 2005), an ambient horn (Price and Rogers, 2004) and the drift table (Gaver et al., 2004) — all of which are unusual, sometimes bizarre and often strange. Gaver et al. (2003) have also argued that ambiguity can be a desirable property in interaction design; making people stop and wonder about the artifact design, and to think more generally about the role technology plays in their lives. The theoretical under-pinning of these forays into more "creative HCI" is that there isn't one preferred interpretation of a system but multiple (Sengers and Gaver, 2006). This way of viewing technology design draws inspiration from Science and Technology Studies (STS), which has documented the many ways that technologies are *interpretively flexible,* i.e., lend themselves to different interpretations besides those intended by their developers (e.g., Bijker, 1995). The idea of framing HCI in the context of multiple interpretations is also behind the cultural theories that have since been imported into HCI, to which we now turn.

6.3   TURN TO CULTURE

There are many questions about how we understand, think, and interpret what we see, hear and touch around us that do not lend themselves to being addressed by scientific theories of cause and effect or social theories of accountability. Many of our concerns about human nature and conduct are about interpretation, such as what did he mean by that, why did he give me that look, why did that performance appear so sublime and so on. These kinds of questions are the bread and butter of other disciplines, namely the Arts and Humanities. They are real questions that invite disciplined answers, involving another language and another conceptual scheme, such as argumentation and intersubjectivity (Scruton, 2012).

There are many theories and approaches within the Arts and Humanities that have evolved to answer questions about the human condition. Several with a background in these fields have jumped ship and joined HCI, as did the sociologists in the 1990s, seeing opportunities to interpret and explain the user experience and other aspects of HCI using their repertoire of interpretative schemes. Cultural theory is one such approach that has made some in-roads into HCI; an umbrella term for social commentary, critical analysis and a re-contextualizing of interaction design (Satchell, 2008). The different disciplines and philosophies they bring to bear include anthropology, social theory, Marxism, feminism, language theory and critical theory. Each of these can be broken down into sub-fields or phases of their development, for example, critical theory comprises film theory, literary theory, political theory and psychoanalytic theory, while feminism has been labeled as liberal, radical, multi-cultural and postmodern among others (Bardzell, 2009). New forms have also been developed to meet the needs of interaction design, namely, *interaction criticism* (Bardzell and Bardzell, 2008).

Critical Theory in a Nutshell

For the outsider, unfamiliar with the landscape of cultural studies, Critical Theory can appear as a dizzying array of perspectives and nuanced varieties. Adopting a critical stance in HCI requires being skeptical, which from a postmodernist position, involves viewing knowledge as subjective construction, being situated in the personal, the social, the conceptual and the political. When applied to user-centered design, it is viewed as the understandings, interpretations and everyday practices of the people being studied or designed for. What this means in practice, is to understand HCI from a number of different angles, such as "linguistic, ideological, gender-based, institutional, environmental" and to develop multi-faceted knowledge constructs that are, "diverse, complex, intentional, subconscious, implicit, genealogically layered, ideological, linguistic and ritually structured — all at once." (Bardzell, 2009).

This seems like an art form and skill set that takes much practice to develop and hone. Indeed, Bardzell et al. (2010) further emphasize how interaction criticism be seen as an *expert reading* of design artifacts, communicating new insights that can be of value to HCI. Part of the expertise in critical practice is knowing the body of knowledge in the design field and having a good sense of the important contributions that can be made from a critical stance. For those unfamiliar with this form of multi-layering and interpretative position, it can appear daunting and unwieldy. As with importing other theories into HCI, there is the danger that, researchers new to critical theory, will cherry pick certain concepts, resulting in them becoming overly simplified when out of context. In doing so, their interpretation — similar to the fate of affordances — may lose their original explanatory force, even to the point of trivializing a topic, and in so doing, making them vulnerable for ridicule by those from other "scientific" schools of thought.

The struggle facing those championing critical theory and, more generally, the adoption of a cultural theory approach to HCI, is what they are offering is an even more radical departure from the scientific paradigm than the Modernist theories imported into HCI. Moreover, bending the underlying principles and ethos of the cultural theory approach to match perceived needs of HCI practice, may be seen by some to be like heresy, grossly distorting its contribution from being interpretative to being other (such as prescriptive). But there is a price to pay for not adapting when decamping into an applied field; critical theorists may be regarded as a fringe activity, and at worse dismissed, by those unfamiliar with their method or style of writing. The way forward has to be to appropriate an HCI-oriented form of interpretation, which is more accessible to the HCI community, but which still has its distinctiveness for addressing questions concerning human nature and the human condition. Bardzell (2009) has made a stab at this, proposing four kinds of mappings that critical theory and aesthetics can make to the practice of HCI: (i) informing the existing design process; (ii) resisting or innovating on the design process; (iii) developing and adapting critical theory relevant for HCI; and (iv) critiquing interaction designs that expose the consequences of design. Significantly, he argues, that such mappings are not intended to supersede or reject previous scientific methods in HCI — as many of the alternative theoretical approaches, such as situated action and ethnomethodology, argued for. This move towards more openness is an important step if it is to survive and flourish in Contemporary HCI, where there are ever more theories popping up, vying for attention.

6.4   TURN TO THE WILD

In-the-wild approaches to interaction design began appearing in the mid-2000s, although Hutchins (1995) seminal book "Cognition in the Wild" set a precedent for rethinking how to study cognitive and social phenomena in context rather than in isolation. Following this significant body of work, a number of in-the-wild studies and accounts began to appear in the HCI and Ubicomp literatures, describing how new technologies were being designed, prototyped, and implemented *in situ* (see Rogers et al., 2007). Wild approaches differ from earlier ethnographic approaches insofar as their focus is not on observing existing practices or deriving system requirements *per se* (Rogers, 2011). Instead, novel technologies are developed to augment people, places and settings; interventions installed and different ways of behaving encouraged. A key concern is to observe how people react, change and integrated these in their everyday lives.

The shift towards conducting in-the-wild studies has largely come about from a growing interest in how pervasive technologies can be designed to enhance and become part of the *everydayness* of life. Instead of the goal being to develop *solutions* that fit in with existing practices, the trend has been to experiment with new technological *possibilities* that can change and even disrupt behavior. Central to designing in-the-wild is being able to show how behavior changes over suitable periods of time of technologies being used *in situ* and in practice.

The outcomes of these in-the-wild studies have been most revealing demonstrating different findings from those arising from studies (Hornecker and Nicol, 2012; Marshall et al., 2011a; Rogers et al., 2007). In particular, in-the-wild studies show how people come to understand and appropriate technologies in their own terms and for their own situated purposes. Another difference is that in the lab participants are brought to the experiment and shown their place by a researcher or assistant and then provided with instructions as to what they have to do. There is always someone at hand to explain the purpose of the study, show how to use the system, or fix things if they don't go according to plan. This form of scaffolding is largely absent in-the-wild. The locus of control shifts from the experimenter to the participant. Hence, it becomes much harder, if not impossible, to design an in-the-wild study that can isolate specific effects. Instead, the researcher has to make sense of data in-the-wild, where there are many factors and interdependencies at play that might be causing the observed effect.

The impact of these studies is making researchers rethink what the role of theory is for in-the-wild. The approach I advocate is to import *different* theories into interaction design that have been developed to explain behavior as it occurs in the real world; and then *re-contextualizing* how such a theory should frame research when used in-the-wild, and ultimately, constructing new *wild theories*, based on the findings from in-the-wild studies (Rogers, 2011).

The first two suggestions resonate with the challenges and approaches the other turns in contemporary HCI are proposing: bringing in alternative theories originating from the behavioral sciences and philosophy — that explain how people behave and act in the real world. One theory is *embodiment* — concerned with the social and physical context of the body in structuring cognition and how the world is experienced (this will be covered in more detail as "a turn" in its own right in the next section). Another is *ecological rationality*, which examines how people can make reasonable decisions given the constraints that they naturally and commonly face, such as limited time, information and computational abilities.

Ecological rationality. There has been a growing interest in how people make decisions when confronted with information overload, such as when shopping on the web or at a store. How easy is it to make a decision when confronted with overwhelming choice? Classical rational theories of decision-making (e.g., von Neumann and Morgenstern, 1944) posit that making a choice involves weighing up the costs and benefits of different courses of action. This is assumed to involve exhaustively processing the information and making trade-offs between features. Such strategies are very costly in computational and informational terms — not least because they require the decision-maker to find a way of comparing the different options.

In contrast, the theory of ecological rationality proposes that people tend to use simple heuristics when making decisions (Gigerenzer et al., 1999). Human minds have evolved to act quickly, making just good enough decisions. This theoretical approach proposes that the mind has adapted its limitations to match the structures of information available in the environment. Instead of trying to process all the available information in the environment and consider all possible options, people often make surprisingly good decisions using simple "fast and frugal" heuristics. These are rules of thumb that ignore most of the available information. They include recognition heuristics that largely eliminate the need for information and just make choices on the basis of what is recognized; search heuristics that look for options only until one is found that is good enough, and choice heuristics that seek as little information as possible to determine which option should be selected. Hence, we typically rely only on a few important cues. For example, in the supermarket, shoppers make snap judgments based on a paucity of information, such as buying brands they recognize, are low-priced, or have attractive packaging — seldom reading other package information. This suggests that an effective design strategy is to follow the adage less is more rather than more is more making key information about a product highly salient.

The theory provides a different way of thinking about designing information and how to make it salient when *in situ*. It goes against the grain of much current thinking in ubiquitous computing about contextual information (often based on unbounded rationality models of decision-making). Instead of providing exhaustive mobile recommenders of restaurants, places to visit, etc., for people on the move, the approach is minimalist, determining how, where and when to display salient information that can be capitalized on as part of a fast and frugal heuristic (Todd et al., 2011). This can lead to thinking about structuring the information environment in subtly different ways that can readily and even unconsciously influence people's choices and behaviors in desired directions. Furthermore, instead of trying to change people's behavior through influencing what and how they consciously think about an issue, it involves thinking about how to change the *context* in which they make their decisions, which may or may not involve conscious decision-making. This has led to quite different ways of designing displays in context in order to depict salient information. Instead of providing ever more information to enable people to compare products when making a choice, it is argued that a better strategy is to design technological interventions that provide just enough information and in the right form to facilitate good choices. One solution is to exploit new forms of augmented reality technology that enable information-frugal decision-making and which have glanceable displays that can represent key information in an easy-to-digest form.

Another idea is to develop new wild theory. But what form should it take? Instead of using theory to make a prediction and applying it to a specific problem, it is argued that a wild theory would address more broadly the interdependences between design, technology and behavior. While using this kind of coarser grain of analysis is not new — for example, socio-technical systems theories have been doing this for years — the subject of interest is, i.e., changing everyday behavior and designing *in situ*. Is so doing, a wild theory would become part of the design discourse rather than being formulated into a specific prediction or explanatory framework.

In-the-wild theory in a Nutshell

A starting point might for developing a wild theory might be a much talked about behavior that society is concerned with (e.g., energy consumption, well being, social entrepreneurship). The focus would be how to augment, facilitate or change it in ways that are desired by individuals and society. The problem-design space is couched in terms of an embodied, ecological or other new theoretical understanding of the way people behave in their everyday world and how a in-the-wild design could change this. A number of couplings between the environment, behavior and technology could be explored. Instead of looking at single cause-effects where doing X will produce Y, we could begin to explore a number of interlinked changes that we wish to implement, some through technological designs and others not. For example, a wild theory of technologically facilitated behavioral change would be concerned with understanding the interdependencies between everyday phenomena, information salience, ubiquitous computing and ethics. Wild theory would also feed directly into the development of conceptual tools for design and research. Hence, I see wild theories as emerging from the cross-fertilization of alternative theory, findings from in-the-wild studies and contemporary social concerns.

6.5   TURN TO EMBODIMENT

The turn to embodiment has been gathering momentum in HCI, following the success of Dourish's (2001) book "Where the Action Is." It is about understanding interaction in terms of practical engagement with the social and physical environment. This is considered to be more representative of the way technology is heading in terms of how it is appropriated by people in their everyday settings and the diversity of physical ways we can now touch, manipulate and use interfaces, from tangibles to gesture-based hands free ones. It draws inspiration from a number of areas and theories, namely, Winograd and Flores's (1986) discussion of phenomenology, Suchman's (1987) notion of situated action, Gibsonian's conception of affordance, philosophical ideas from Heidegger (1996) thesis about "embodied interaction." That is a lot of ideas to bring together! Instead of trying to be a unified overarching theory, it has been suggested that it is more profitable to consider using the different aspects of embodiment to account for different behaviors (Marshall et al., 2013); for example, in describing what actions are available in a physically shared space (Robertson, 1997) and encouraging students to learn through physical manipulations or movements (Antle et al., 2009).

Embodied Interaction in a Nutshell

To adopt an embodied interaction stance means having a particular sensibility and approach to viewing technology, design and the world. An embodied interaction perspective takes account of the way human beings are embodied, where perception and action are always embodied. This allows for viewing interactions differently from viewing perception and action as separate stages. Dourish (2001) proposed embodied interaction essentially as a *stance* and *an organizing principle* that researchers and designers can adopt to help them uncover issues in the design and use of existing technologies and the design of new interactive systems. Everyday practices can be examined, analyzed and critiqued in relation to principles, claims and arguments about embodiment. The latter include "technology and practice cannot be separated from each other; they are coextensive and will coevolve," "embodied interaction turns action into meaning" and "meanings arise on multiple levels."

Different meanings are ascribed in interaction through our embodied inter-action with the tangible world and with each other. Rather than struggle to make sense of the inflexible meaning encoded in computers we create and communicate meaning of our actions by exploring, adapting and adopting in-teractive technologies, incorporating it into our world and everyday practices. For example, an interactive surface can be at once, a tool to plan a day out, a shared space that a group can gather around in discussion, and a convenient surface on which to place a cup of coffee.

For some, reading Dourish's book can be enlightening, setting them off in new research directions. Others, however, have struggled to understand the connotations of what an embodied stance means and how to go about operationalizing it. Klemmer et al. (2006) have tried to fill this gap by developing a more applied framework of embodiment, suggesting a number of concrete themes intended to help designers. Similar to Dourish and others, they draw from a variety of theoretical and empirical works to explain embodiment; but their particular flavor draws from a synthesis of ideas arising out of philosophy, psychology and sociology, resulting in a theoretical blending that promotes bodily engagement with the physical and digital worlds; tangibility and reflective practice. In contrast to Dourish's take on embodiment, they emphasize the impact of *learning through doing*; drawing ideas from developmental psychology theory about how children learn to move their bodies and the consequences of their actions. They outline five themes intended to *inspire* new design approaches that combine the physical with the computational and also as input for evaluating systems in context.

While the five themes summarize succinctly a body of relevant theoretical and empirical research, together with raising new questions, they, too, only really hint at how the designer might consider different facets of "thinking through doing." The extent to which a designer or researcher can apply one or more of these themes ultimately depends on their sensibilities to the underlying philosophy. Hence, similar to Dourish's stance, they still have to do the work "to work out" what it means to design *embodied* technologies for *embodied* people in an *embedded* world.

Another more applied approach to embodied interaction is Hornecker and Buur's (2006) Tangible Interaction framework that conceptualizes technologies in terms of embodied interaction, tangible manipulation, physical representation of data and embeddedness in real space. It offers four themes and a set of concepts intended to help researchers in understanding the interaction with tangible interaction systems and in designing for the support of social interaction. These are *tangible manipulation* (the material representations with distinct tactile qualities), *spatial interaction* (it is embedded in real space and therefore occurs by movement in space), *embodied facilitation* (how the configuration of material objects and space affects and directs emerging group behavior) and *expressive representation* (the expressiveness and legibility of tangible systems). Similar to Klemmer et al. (2006) their framework leaves it to designers' interpretation and sensibilities, but tries to summarize the main issues as questions that can drive and inspire creative design.

As with the cultural theory approaches, there is a danger that such under-specificity — be it Dourish, Klemmer et al. or Hornecker and Buur's take on embodiment — might result, yet again, in a piecemeal approach where the researcher or designer, finds themselves slipping into over-simplified interpretations of embodiment, that bear little resemblance with the phenomenological experience of enactment. When everyone starts talking about: "embodied this, embodied that" it will be like Norman's affordances, where everyone is referring to a sense of body-interaction, but not much more. But, clearly, theories about embodiment and their implications for design are more than skin deep. The question this raises is whether it really matters if people talk about embodied this or embodied that when they mean something less than envisioned by those who have imported and re-interpreted it in an HCI context. If it adds to their armory of terms, and importantly, others understand what they mean by it, then it seems a harmless addition.

A different approach has been to show how the idea of embodiment can be specifically applied. Instead of blending theories, a single theoretical framework is used to directly inform the design of interfaces — in some ways not dissimilar to the Classical theory approach. An example is Hurtienne's (2009) approach; he has drawn inspiration from cognitive linguistics, leading to a new cognitive theory in interaction design. His theory of embodied cognition is grounded in the ways that people experience the world through physical interaction, and it emphasizes the value of using abstraction from specific contexts. In particular, he draws from *image schema theory* (Johnson, 1987) that describes the *abstract representations of recurring sensorimotor patterns of experience*. An example of an image schema is when we place objects in other ones; it leads to a higher-level understanding of what a "container" is and its attributes (e.g., an inside, a boundary, an outside, one can be placed inside another).

Based on the ideas from schema image, Hurtienne (2009) designed different interfaces that he then made predictions about in terms of user. The findings from his experiments show both preference and performance being better for interfaces that map onto the schema than those that are inconsistent with them. He suggests that image schemas could be usefully employed as part of the language to describe conceptual models (cf. Johnson and Henderson, 2012) while also offering a way of showing how a cognitive linguistic theory of embodiment can be practically applied to interface design that is suggestive but also flexible.

6.6 THE NEXT TURN

I have described a number of turns that have taken place during the most recent period of HCI, and outlined some of the contemporary theories that have emerged. Many of these have been aligned with the third-wave HCI (Harrison et al., 2011, 2007). My intention, here, has been to focus on the theoretical developments that have spanned the history of HCI, their promise and impact. My three proposed epochs were shown to have parallels with the three main periods labeled in the history of Art: Classical, Modern and Contemporary. There is of course overlap with the way the three waves have been defined and distinguished in critiques and overviews of HCI; however, the three terms used here offer further distinguishing features that are specific to the way theory has emerged, evolved and exited.

It is impossible to do justice to all the theories that have been promulgated and published in the burgeoning HCI literature. As I write, there are other theories beginning to make their mark, that some might consider warrant being labeled as another turn. For example, there is the beginnings of a "turn to space," that includes schematic modeling frameworks, such as *proxemics* and *F-formations*, which conceptualise people's everyday interactions with each other in physical space, using diagrammatic formats that lend themselves to doing some of the "the work" that designers need to do, especially as they broaden out to address design in terms of expanding technologies, environments and values. Both of these schematic frameworks were developed for analyzing social interactions and have been shown to be highly relevant to recent technology design concerns — such as people's expectations and understanding of how an ecology of devices and displays should behave when embedded in the environment while also being part of their own set of personal devices. Proxemics, originally developed by the cultural anthropologist Edward Hall (1963), is concerned with how people interpret and use spatial relationships in their everyday lives with a focus on the use of space in interpersonal communication. Parallels are drawn when thinking about the design of device ecologies (Ballendat et al., 2010): just as people expect more engagement and intimacy when they move closer to others, so will they expect more interaction possibilities with the devices and displays they come into closer contact with. F-formations, originally developed by Adam Kendon (1990), is concerned with analyzing how the spatial organization and physical aspects of a setting influence interactions between people. In essence, they are the spatial patterns formed during face-to-face interactions between two or more people. Marshall et al. (2011b) showed how it can be applied to understanding how different kinds of technology-embedded/rich environments can constrain social interactions and how this can feed into the design of shared technologies, where the aim is to transform the social interactions.

Within art history, there are ongoing debates about where next; post post-modernism, post neo, and post contemporary and so on. The relentless striving for the new, coupled with an ever increasing self-awareness, suggests the new kids on the block will always want to create new movements, but the problem for them is what to call them (since all the "new" words have all but been exhausted) and how they will differ from previous ones (since there are fewer ideas and framings that have not been conceived of before). One suggestion is that the art world can go backwards as easily as forwards: "all of a sudden the mechanisms of previous novelties are called upon and pushed out to center stage, redressed" (Bradley, 2011). The same fate may fall upon HCI theory, too, where researchers continue wrestling with "out with the old/in with the new," but the difference being, that each new generation of Young Turks has to fight within an increasingly crowded space. Retro theory might just become the old-new.

CHAPTER 7

Discussion

Theory weary, theory leery,
why can't I be theory cheery? (Tom Erickson, 2002).

My overview of the history of the "theory industry" in HCI and its diversification has shown, on the one hand, it to have been successful in shaping research but on the other, less impressive in being applied in practice. Clearly, it continues to play an important role in framing and moving the HCI research agenda forward but the chasm between theory and practice, identified early on in HCI (e.g., Landauer, 1991; Long, 1991) persists. Below, I explore the reasons for this and argue that, perhaps, the theory-practice divide could be bridged better, through rethinking how to develop HCI theory that can assimilate the messy and ever-changing, technologically augmented world.

Table 7.1 provides an overall summary of the different roles theory has been developed for in HCI. These are not meant to be mutually exclusive (and some do overlap) but to show the different ways that theory has and can play, as promoted by researchers in the Classical, Modern and Contemporary periods.

Table 7.1: A summary of the ways theory has been used and developed in HCI

Kind	Description
Descriptive	Clarifying terminology and guiding inquiry
Explanatory	Explicating relationships and processes
Predictive	Testing hypotheses about user performance
Prescriptive	Providing guidance on how best to design and evaluate
Informative	Importing relevant findings to ground understanding of HCI
Ethnographic	Providing detailed descriptions arising from a field study
Conceptual	Eliciting frameworks for informing design and evaluation
Critical	Couching HCI in a cultural and aesthetic context
Wild	Developing new theories of technology use *in situ*

7.1 MOST SUCCESSFUL

One of the most prolific and, arguably, successful developments in and applications of HCI theory has been conceptual frameworks, derived from an imported theory (or set of theories), the synthesis of empirical research (ethnographic, experimental and case study), design practice or a set of assumptions about the structure and/or function of phenomena. Unlike the design implications approach, whose value has been questioned by researchers, the conceptual frameworks approach has been received favorably in the HCI community. Frameworks often are the driving force that run through a research project, being the accumulation of a body of theorizing and empirical work, and which are illustrated by cases studies showing how they have been generalized and applied.

Conceptual frameworks can vary along a continuum of prescription-explanation: the more prescriptive a framework the more likely it will consist of a series of steps or principles to be followed. The more explanatory a framework, the more likely it will consist of a set of concepts or dimensions to be considered. Benford et al. (2009) propose a number of ways conceptual frameworks can be used from their research, including compiling and analyzing the extensive craft knowledge that already exists among artists and other designers, and helping technology researchers and developers identify requirements for new tools and platforms to support the development and orchestration of future user experiences. Evidence of the success of conceptual frameworks can be counted in the reporting by others of having used them in different projects, and ideally case studies of them being used in practice. The latter are less forthcoming, as practitioners have to eke out a living from consulting and often do not have the time or funding to publish their work (but see the set of case studies at id-book.com). There are, however, a number of frameworks that have been well cited in the literature, for example, Bellotti and Edwards (2001) context-aware framework, outlining principles of intelligibility and accountability; Bellotti et al.'s (2002) making sense of sensing systems framework explicating challenges, design issues and problems; Benford et al.'s (2009) interactional trajectories, which is a sensitizing framework for understanding cultural experiences, in museums, mixed reality games, etc., as journeys through hybrid structures, punctuated by transitions, and in which interactivity and collaboration are orchestrated; and Gaver et al.'s (2003) ambiguity framework, comprising a set of tactics for designing ambiguous representations, artifacts and situations aimed at getting people to interpret them differently. Interestingly, these frameworks have been largely prescriptive in their design advice, suggesting what to do (or not to do) — for example, Benford et al. (2005) recommend that designers "identify all known limitations of the sensing technologies, by considering range, speed, accuracy and stability of sensing."

Rogers and Muller's (2006) framework of sensor-based interactions was meant more as an articulatory device helping to define and shape user experiences. Instead of being prescriptive, it conceptualizes a number of core dimensions of sensors together with aspects of the user experience that are considered important to take into account when designing sensor-based interactions. The framework is intended to help designers, interested in developing innovative playful learning experiences that use sensor-based interaction (as opposed to GUI interaction) but aren't sure about how to put them to novel and innovative effect. There are many possibilities available to designers when deciding which sensor technology to couple with which system response (and how). However, the new generation of sensing technologies (e.g., motion, light, pressure) can be problematic in what they can detect and how they detect it. The framework was proposed in recognition of this and to enable designers to explore how to exploit to good effect these new kinds of interactions.

More recently, Yuill and Rogers (2012) developed the "Mechanisms for Collaboration" conceptual framework, that presents the core psychological and behavioral mechanisms that are thought to underlie the successes of shared interfaces for collaboration and which are intended to be considered in conjunction with various kinds of physical, technological and social constraints, derived from a combined analysis of theory in the fields of Developmental Psychology and Ubicomp, and reflecting on everyday interactions. The framework is intended to help designers and researchers think about *multiple* concerns and dependencies when designing shared technologies. Rather than asking, "How do I design a multitouch surface or a natural user interface that will enhance cooperation or collaboration?" it suggests reconceptualizing this research question to become "What is the interplay between the various behavioral mechanisms for the proposed activity and setting?" For example, it suggests considering how to make obvious the way in which one should behave and how to give appropriate cues, as well as how to make more salient the cues that can lead to improved understanding, explication of intentions, and focus of attention. Hence, the aim is to provide a principled way for researchers and designers to make sense of the emerging empirical literature on the benefits of multi-user interfaces and to understand how they will be used in real-world contexts.

Ethnographic approaches have also stood their ground, making a significant contribution to the body of HCI knowledge, addressing Plowman et al.'s (1995) earlier concern: "what are work studies for?" The recent debates, outlined in Chapter 4, concerning how they should be framed, interpreted and applied have also highlighted both their successes and limitations.

7.2   SOMEWHAT LESS SUCCESSFUL

Many of the theoretically based concepts promoted in HCI, that were drawn from a variety of disciplines have largely fallen by the wayside, while a few have become common parlance. For example, the notions of affordances and context are those that have stuck and become mainstream while concepts such as mental models and cognitive dimensions, while popular to begin with, are no longer fashionable. Despite having much currency, the latter proved a step too far for designers (and others) to become sufficiently versed in to be able to talk about design issues with each other using such terms, as viscosity. One of the reasons is the effort required to learn them — even the basic set of 12. It seems akin to asking people to learn a new language late on in life, such as Esperanto, which if everyone learnt it, it would be great, greatly increasing our capacity for articulating design concerns. We would have shared references and would not spend countless hours aligning what we each mean by our nuanced meanings of common terms such as representation, platform and process. Instead, it seems stand-alone, one-off terms that conjure up what they mean intuitively have been the most widely taken up — even though they are often used much more loosely and in underspecified ways.

7.3   NOT SO SUCCESSFUL

Where imported theories have been least successful is when adapted as generalizable methods (i.e., the prescriptive and predictive categories), intended to be used by practitioners. The reasons for this lack of uptake are wide-ranging, and need to be taken into account in the wider context of applying theory in practice. Firstly, it must be stressed that it is foolish to assume or hope that theories "do design," however much the proponents of the theoretical approach would like (Barnard and May, 1999). Their input to the design process can only ever really be indirect, in the form of providing methods, concepts and analytic tools. A theory cannot provide prescriptive guidance in the sense of literally telling a designer what and how to do design. The contribution of any theory must be viewed sensibly and in the context of its role in the design process at large.

Secondly, designers already have their own established craft methods to use as well as practical interaction design techniques (e.g., prototyping, heuristic evaluation, scenario-based design). For this reason, the value of theory-informed methods must be seen in relation to current design practice — and which is why Benford et al.'s family of conceptual frameworks has often fared better than others, as they have tended to graft onto existing practice.

Thirdly, more time is needed to allow a complete theory/design cycle to mature (see Plowman et al., 1995) and show impact in the field (through paper citation and download-ing, and successful products being built based on them). It may take several years before we see more success stories being reported in the literature — just as it took several years after GOMS was developed before its value in a real work setting was reported.

Fourthly, considerable time, effort and skill are required by many of the approaches to un-derstand and know how to use them. In particular, many require a background or training in the mother discipline to truly understand its ramifications for HCI. Ethnographic fieldwork is now often required as part of an approach. Knowing how to "do" ethnography and to interpret the findings in relation to a theoretical framework (e.g., ethnomethodology, distributed cognition, cultural theory) is a highly skilled activity that requires extensive training and much painstaking analysis. It is hard to learn and become competent at: many a student in HCI, has been attracted by the ethnographic approach and the theoretical framework of distributed cognition, only to find themselves, in the midst of a field study, surrounded by masses of "raw" video data without any real sense of what to look for or how to analyze the data in terms of, say, 'propagation of representational state across media."

More generally, there is little consensus as to what contribution the various approaches can or should make to interaction design. The transfer vehicles that became the standard and generally accepted "deliverables" and "products'" for informing design during the 1980s (e.g., design principles and guidelines, style books, predictable and quantifiable models) are regarded as inadequate or inappropriate for translating the kinds of critical writings and detailed accounts that recent theoretical approaches imported into HCI have to offer. There is also less evident, a rhetoric of compassion (Cooper, 1991), where researchers from one community try to articulate what needs to be done in another community.

The analytic frameworks that were proposed, such as those derived from Activity Theory, have also suffered from being under-specified, making it difficult for researchers and designers to know whether the way one is using them is appropriate and has validity. This contrasts with the application of earlier cognitive theories to HCI, where the prescribed route outlined by the scientific method was typically followed (i.e., make hypotheses, carry out experiment to test them, determine if hypotheses are supported or repudiated, develop theory further, repeat procedure). Without the rigor and systematicity of the scientific method at hand, it is more difficult to know how to use them to best effect or whether what they come up with can be validated.

A further problem from both the designer's and researcher's perspective, is that there is now a large and ever increasing number of theoretical approaches vying with each other, making it more difficult for them to determine which is potentially most useful for them or, indeed, how to use one with respect to their own specific research or design concerns. Such a confusing state of affairs has been recognized in the HCI community and one or two attempts have been made to synthesize and make sense of the medley of approaches. For example, Nardi (1996) sought to compare and contrast selected approaches in terms of their merits and differences for system design. However, given that the various approaches have widely differing epistemologies, ontologies and methods such comparative analyses can only ever really scratch the surface. There is also the problem that this kind of exercise can end up similar to comparing apples and oranges — whereby it becomes impossible, if not illogical to judge disparate approaches (cf. Patel and Groen, 1993).

7.4   MOVING THEORY FORWARD: NEW FRAMINGS

As was seen in the previous chapters on HCI theory, a common practice has been to dismiss a dominant approach and replace it with a new research agenda, epistemology and framing of the research. This was a particularly popular tactic in Modern HCI theory. However, championing one theoretical approach over another often ends up being a matter of personal preference, stemming from one's own background and values as to what constitutes good design practice or research. At worst it can end up as a bun fight, where tempers flare and criticism becomes personal and even derogatory. That is not to say that one cannot highlight the strengths and weaknesses of a particular approach so long as it is constructive criticism.

Another way forward is to consider whether different epistemologies and frames of references can complement each other. The arrival of the situated action approach on the scene in the late 1980s illustrates this. Clancey (1993), originally a traditional AI researcher, became a convert with the turn to the social arguing how situated action made him think more about the language used in the classical theories of HCI, namely, "memory," "knowledge," "information," "symbol," "representation" and "plan." In terms of whether they should be abandoned in favor of new ones, such as context, situatedness, and contingency, he argued that while they suggest a new research agenda, it is not necessary to break away completely from traditional theories. Instead, he proposed reconsidering the relation of cognitive models to the phenomena that they were intended to explicate.

But some researchers revel in the rhetoric of dismissing other perspectives, where much of their stance is in criticizing the problems, limitations and flaws of anothers' approach. More recently, however, the zeitgeist has been towards more tolerance of other theoretical positions, suggesting that they can sit side-by-side (e.g., Bardzell, 2009) and be synthesized in novel ways (Rogers, 2011). Bannon (2011a) has also called for a re-imagining of HCI by encouraging more openness to new forms of thinking about human-technology relationships.

Table 7.2 highlights what a more open HCI might be like and the role theory would play (Rogers, 2009). It contrasts past concerns with future ones along four dimensions. Firstly,

Table 7.2: Framing past and future concerns for HCI (Based on Rogers, 2009)		
Concern	Past	Future
Frame of reference	• users	• context
Method, theory, and perspective	• scientific approach	• pluralistic
	• interaction design	• mixing
Outputs	• ethnographies•	• insights
	• models and tools for analysis	•• creating new ways of experiencing•
	•• design guidance	• value-based analyses

in terms of a frame of reference, it suggests that the focus of HCI shift from "the user" to embrace a wider context. This is already happening, with many researchers being preoccupied with personal, social and cultural aspects of technology use and augmentation as much as user's needs. Secondly, it notes how the methods, theory and perspective of HCI have in the past followed either the scientific approach (e.g., conducting experiments based on cognitive theory and doing user testing) or inter-action design (e.g., prototyping, user studies, ethnography) and is being replaced with a multiple and hybrid methodology (including running experiments and doing ethnography together) that previ-ously might have been considered incommensurate, but which are being mixed and even mashed in order to probe and analyze the wider and sometimes elusive set of concerns. Thirdly, it suggests that the current way of working together inspired by interdisciplinarity, is making way for various forms of transdisciplinarity. The "trans" refers to integrative knowledge based on the convergence of concepts and methods from different research areas, including computing, philosophy, psychology, art and design, ethics and engineering. It involves moving between the big picture and the details of a research question, using a combination of strategies, design methods and theories. For example, this could involve the application of philosophical theory to technological innovation, where conceptual philosophical analysis is fed into the design process and the experiences of being engaged in user studies are fed back into the philosophical analyses. In summary, transdisciplinarity is an approach that focuses on a broader goal: transcending disciplinarity and using collections of theories and their associated bodies of knowledge as and when deemed appropriate — which is well suited to HCI and the practice of interaction design (Blevis and Stolterman, 2009). Fourthly, whereas in the past, outputs from HCI research and practice have been either design implications or rich descriptions from ethnographic research; models of the user or the user experience; or conceptual and evaluative tools for analysis, it suggests that future outputs will demonstrate how to develop user experiences and human augmentation that covers a range of human values.

CHAPTER 8

Summary

"Theories are more like a pair of dark glasses. We put them on and the world is tinted. The change brings some objects into sharper contrast, while others fade into obscurity." (Christine Halverson, 2002, p245)

So what next for HCI theory? Given the various problems that have been identified when moving between theory and practice, might we be better off by abandoning the theory industry in HCI and letting interaction design evolve more as an applied field, where new methods and approaches — based on practice rather than abstraction — increasingly lead the field? After all, many popular methods, innovative interfaces and design solutions have been developed without a whisker of a theory in sight. On the other hand, it would surely be a shame to throw the baby out with the bath water. Theory can be very powerful in advancing knowledge in a field.

Many researchers already have moved on from the theory-practice debates that were so central to the Classical and Modernist periods of HCI theory development. They are much more motivated by addressing societal goals and the difficult challenges of big HCI, and are happy to use whatever methods come to hand to enable them to deal with more open-ended tasks, community relationships, policy negotiation and conflict resolution. Other dilemmas are replacing them, however. For example, for those who are working in the area of ICT4D, there is the tension of trying to help a community through "developing" and implementing an appropriate technology versus trying to make a new contribution to the field so that they can get published — after all they are funded as researchers. Many weeks, months and years can be spent by a team of researchers, to establish a new technology infrastructure that can help a local village collect water more efficiently, only for it not to be deemed methodologically rigorous enough for it to warrant publication at a CHI conference!

At the other end of the spectrum, are those who have moved into core computer science areas or nouvelle AI, where machine learning, big data and sensor networks are the order of the day, and the contribution is in the quantifying, combining and analyzing of algorithms and data in order to model and visualize new forms of human behavior.

My own view is that theory importing and building will continue to play an important role in HCI. The battles that were fought and the gallant, but often in vain, efforts to bridge the theory-practice divide already seem like a distant past. Instead, we are beginning to learn to be tolerant, open and transdisciplinary. As a result, in the future we will develop broader discourses, conversing with ever more fields, embracing the big and small, creating new theories in-the-wild that ultimately, can make an impact on society, at many levels. Theory may even lead practice rather than lagging behind it. As we continue to cast our nets further afield, theoretical posturing will diminish, making place for healthy theoretical debates about social responsibility, generalization and abstraction.

Bibliography

Ackerman, M. and Halverson, C. (1998) Considering an organization's memory. In *Proc. of Computer-Supported Cooperative Work, CSCW'98*, ACM, New York, 39–48. DOI: 10.1145/289444.289461 Cited on page(s) 39

Anderson, R.J. (1994) Representations and requirements: The value of ethnography. In system design. *Human Computer Interaction* 9, 151–182. DOI: 10.1207/s15327051hci0902_1 Cited on page(s) 32, 48

Anderson, R., Button, G. and Sharrock, W. (1993) Supporting the design process within an organizational context. *Proc. of 3rd ECSCW.* Kluwer Academic Press, 47–59. Cited on page(s) 49

Antle, A.N., Corness, G. and Droumeva, M. (2009) Human-computer-intuition? Exploring the cognitive basis for intuition in embodied interaction. *International Journal of Arts and Technology* 2(3), 235–254. DOI: 10.1504/IJART.2009.028927 Cited on page(s) 76

Artman, H. and Waern, Y. (1999) Distributed cognition in an emergency Co-ordination Center. *Cognition, Technology and Work* 1, 237–246. DOI: 10.1007/s101110050020 Cited on page(s) 39

Ashton, K. (2009) That 'Internet of Things' thing. *RFID Journal* 22. Cited on page(s) 12

Atwood, M.E., Gray, W.D. and John, B.E. (1996) Project Ernestine: Analytic and empirical methods applied to a real world CHI problem. In Rudisill, M., Lewis, C., Polson, P. and McKay, T.D., Eds., *Human Computer Interface Design: Success Stories, Emerging Methods and Real World Context.* Morgan Kaufmann, San Francisco, CA, 101–121. Cited on page(s) 26

Austin, J.L. (1962) *How to do Things with Words: The William James Lectures delivered at Harvard University in 1955.* Urmson, J. O., Ed., Clarendon, Oxford. Cited on page(s) 53

Badiou, A. (1988) *Being and Event.* trans O. Feltham. Continuum. Cited on page(s) 69

Bailey, B. (2000) How to improve design decisions by reducing reliance on superstition. Let's start with Miller's Magic 7+−2. *Human Factors International, Inc.,* Downloaded from www.humanfactors.com Cited on page(s) 22

Ballendat, T., Marquardt, N. and Greenberg, S. (2010) Proxemic interaction: Designing for a proximity and orientation-aware environment. *Proc. of ITS'10: International Conference on Interactive Tabletops and Surfaces*, 121–130. DOI: 10.1145/1936652.1936676 Cited on page(s) 14, 79

Bannon, L. (2011a) Re-framing HCI: from human-computer interaction to human-centred inter-action design. *Proc. CHItaly'11*, 17–18. DOI: 10.1145/2037296.2037304 Cited on page(s) 1, 12, 86

Bannon, L. (2011b) Reimagining HCI: toward a more human-centered perspective. *Interactions* 18(4), 50–57. DOI: 10.1145/1978822.1978833 Cited on page(s) 12, 13

Bannon, L. and Bødker, S. (1991) Encountering artefacts in use. In Carroll, J., Ed., *Designing Interaction: Psychology at the Human-Computer Interface*. Cambridge University Press, New York, 27–253. Cited on page(s) 31, 32, 55

Bardzell, J. (2009) Interaction criticism and aesthetics. *Proc. CHI'09*, ACM, 2357–2366. DOI: 10.1145/1518701.1519063 Cited on page(s) 71, 72, 73, 86

Bardzell, J. and Bardzell, S. (2008) Interaction criticism: A proposal and framework for a new discipline of HCI. In *CHI'08 Extended Abstracts*, ACM, 2463–2472. DOI: 10.1145/1358628.1358703 Cited on page(s) 71

Bardzell, J. and Bardzell, S. (2011) Pleasure is your birthright: digitally enabled designer sex toys as a case of third-wave HCI. *Proc. CHI'11*, ACM, 257–266. DOI: 10.1145/1978942.1978979 Cited on page(s) xi

Bardzell, J., Bolter, J. and Löwgren, J. (2010) Interaction criticism: Three readings of an interaction design and what they get us. *Interactions* 14. DOI: 10.1145/1699775.1699783 Cited on page(s) 72

Barley, S., Kiesler, S., Kraut, R.E., Dutton, W.H., Resnick, P. and Yates, J. (2004) Does CSCW need organization theory. *Proc. of CSCW'04*, ACM, 122–124. DOI: 10.1145/1031607.1031628 Cited on page(s) 16

Barnard, P. (1991) Bridging between basic theories and the artefacts of human-computer interaction. In Carroll, J., Ed., *Designing Interaction: Psychology at the Human-Computer Interface*. Cambridge University Press, New York, 103–127. Cited on page(s) 31

Barnard, P.J. and May, J. (1999) Representing cognitive activity in complex tasks. *Human-Computer Interaction* 14, 93–158. DOI: 10.1207/s15327051hci1401&2_4 Cited on page(s) 31, 84

Barnard, P.J., Hammond, N., Maclean, A. and Morten, J. (1982) Learning and remembering interactive commands in a text editing task. *Behaviour and Information Technology* 1, 347–358. DOI: 10.1080/01449298208914458 Cited on page(s) 23

Barnard, P.J., May, J., Duke, D.J. and Duce, D.A. (2000) Systems interactions and macrotheory. *Transactions On Computer Human Interaction* 7, 222–262. DOI: 10.1145/353485.353490 Cited on page(s) 1, 13, 15, 63

Bederson, B. and Shneiderman, B. (Eds.) (2003) *The Craft of Information Visualization: Readings and Reflections.* Morgan Kaufmann, San Francisco, CA. Cited on page(s) 16

Bell, G., Blythe, M., Gaver, B., Sengers, P. and Wright, P.C. (2003) Designing culturally situated technologies for the home. *Proc. CHI'03 Extended Abstracts*, ACM, 1062–1063. DOI: 10.1145/765891.766149 Cited on page(s) 66

Bell, G. and Dourish, P. (2007) Yesterday's tomorrows: notes on ubiquitous computing's dominant vision. *Personal and Ubiquitous Comput.* 11(2), 133–143. DOI: 10.1007/s00779-006-0071-x Cited on page(s) 11

Bellotti, V. and Edwards, K. (2001) Intelligibility and accountability: human considerations in context-aware systems. *Human-Computer Interaction* 16(2), 193–212. DOI: 10.1207/S15327051HCI16234_05 Cited on page(s) 82

Bellotti, V., Back, M.J., Edwards, W.K., Grinter, R.E., Lopes, C.V. and Henderson, A. (2002) Making sense of sensing systems: Five questions for designers and researchers. *Proc. of CHI'02*, ACM, 415–422. DOI: 10.1145/503376.503450 Cited on page(s) 82

Benford, S., Schädelbach, H., Koleva, B., Anastasi, R., Greenhalgh, C., Rodden, T., Green, J., Ghali, A., Pridmore, T., Gaver, B., Boucher, A., Walker, B., Pennington, S., Schmidt, A., Gellersen, H. and Steed, A. (2005) Expected, sensed, and desired: A framework for designing sensing-based interaction. *ACM Transactions on Computer-Human Interaction* 12(1), 3–30. DOI: 10.1145/1057237.1057239 Cited on page(s) 82

Benford, S., Giannachi, G., Koleva, B. and Rodden, T. (2009) From interaction to trajectories: Designing coherent journeys through user experiences. *Proc. of CHI'09*, ACM, 709–718. DOI: 10.1145/1518701.1518812 Cited on page(s) 82

Bentley, R., Hughes J.A., Randall, D., Rodden, T., Sawyer, P., Sommerville, I. and Shapiro, D. (1992) Ethnographically-informed systems design for air traffic control. *Proc. of CSCW'92*, ACM, 123–129. DOI: 10.1145/143457.143470 Cited on page(s) 48

Beyer, H. and Holtzblatt, K. (1998) *Contextual Design: Customer-Centered Systems.* Morgan Kauffman, San Francisco, CA. Cited on page(s) 40, 41

Bijker, W.E. (1995) *Of Bicycles, Bakelites and Bulbs: Toward a Theory of Sociotechnical Change.* MIT Press, Cambridge, MA. Cited on page(s) 71

Blackwell, A.F. and Green, T.R.G. (2000) A cognitive dimensions questionnaire optimised for users. In Blackwell, A.F. and Bilotta, E., Eds., *Proc. of Twelfth Annual Meeting of the Psychology of Programming Interest Group (PPIG-12)* 1(2), 137–152. Cited on page(s) 36

Blandford, A. and Furniss, D. (2005) DiCoT: A methodology for applying Distributed Cognition to the design of team working systems. *Proc. DSVIS2005.* Springer: LNCS. DOI: 10.1007/11752707_3 Cited on page(s) 40

Blevis, E. (2007) Sustainable interaction design: Invention and disposal, renewal and reuse. *Proc. CHI'07,* ACM, 503–512. DOI: 10.1145/1240624.1240705 Cited on page(s) 69

Blevis, E. and Stolterman, E. (2009) Transcending disciplinary boundaries in interaction design. *Interactions* 16(5), 48–51. DOI: 10.1145/1572626.1572636 Cited on page(s) 87

Bly, S. (1997) Field work: Is it product work? *Interactions,* January and February, 25–30. DOI: 10.1145/242388.242398 Cited on page(s) 47

Blythe, M., Bardzell, J., Bardzell, S. and Blackwell, A. (2008) Critical issues in Interaction Design. *Proc. of British HCI 2008.* Cited on page(s) 12, 65

Bødker, S. (1989) A human activity approach to user interfaces. *Human Computer Interaction* 4(3), 171–195. Cited on page(s) 55

Bødker, S. (2006) When second wave HCI meets third wave challenges. In *Proc. of the 4th Nordic Conf. on Human-Computer Interaction: Changing Roles (NordiCHI'06),* ACM, New York, 1–8. DOI: 10.1145/1182475.1182476 Cited on page(s) 7, 12

Borgmann, A. (1992) *Crossing the Postmodern Divide.* University of Chicago Press, Chicago. Cited on page(s) 69

Bradley, R.D. (2011) Novelty and Whatever Comes Next After Contemporary Art. Downloaded on 20/2/12 from `http://pooool.info/uncategorized/novelty-whatever-comes-next-after-contemporary-art/` Cited on page(s) 79

Button, G. (Ed.) (1993) *Technology in Working Order.* Routledge, London. Cited on page(s) 32

Button, G. (1997) Book review: Cognition in the Wild. *CSCW* 6, 391–395. Cited on page(s) 40

Button, G. (2003) Studies of work in human computer interaction. In Carroll, J.M., Ed., *HCI Models, Theories, and Frameworks: Towards a Multidisciplinary Science.* Morgan Kaufmann Publishers, San Francisco, CA, 357–380. Cited on page(s) 45, 49

Button, G. and Dourish, P. (1996) Technomethodology: Paradoxes and possibilities. *Proc. of CHI'96,* ACM, 19–26. DOI: 10.1145/238386.238394 Cited on page(s) 47, 49

Card, S.K., Moran, T.P. and Newell, A. (1983) *The Psychology of Human-Computer Interaction.* Hillsdale, LEA, Hillsdale, NJ. Cited on page(s) 24, 25

Carroll, J. (2003) Introduction: Toward a multidisciplinary science of human-computer interaction. In Carroll, J.M., Ed., *HCI Models, Theories and Frameworks*. Morgan Kaufmann, San Francisco, CA. Cited on page(s) 2, 4

Carroll, J.M. (Ed.) (1991) *Designing Interaction: Psychology at the Human-Computer Interface*. Cambridge University Press, Cambridge. Cited on page(s) 21, 31

Carroll, J.M., Kellogg, W.A. and Rosson, M.B. (1991) The task-artifact cycle. In Carroll, J.M., Ed., *Designing Interaction: Psychology at the Human-Computer Interface*. Cambridge University Press, Cambridge, 74–102. Cited on page(s) 31

Castell, F. (2002) Theory, theory on the wall…, *CACM* 45, 25–26. *Cognitive Science* 18, 87–122. Cited on page(s) 13

Chalmers, M. (2008) Forward in A. Clark. *Supersizing the Mind*. Oxford University Press, Oxford. Cited on page(s) 10

Charmaz, K. (2011) Grounded theory methods in social justice research. In Denzin, N.K. and Lincoln, Y.E., Eds., *Handbook of Qualitative Research*, 4th ed., Sage, Thousand Oaks, CA. Cited on page(s) 61, 62

Clancey, W.J. (1993) Situated action: A neuropsychological interpretation response to Vera and Simon. *Cognitive Science* 17, 87–116. DOI: 10.1207/s15516709cog1701_7 Cited on page(s) 47, 85

Clark, A. (2004) *Natural Born Cyborgs*. Oxford University Press, Oxford. Cited on page(s) 9, 15

Cockton, G. (2006) Designing worth is worth designing. *Proc. NORDCHI*, ACM, 165–174. DOI: 10.1145/1182475.1182493 Cited on page(s) 69

Cockton, G. (2010) Design situations and methodological innovation in interaction design. *Proc. CHI'10 Extended Abstracts*, 2745–2754. DOI: 10.1145/1753846.1753859 Cited on page(s) 69

Collins, P., Shulka, S. and Redmiles, D. (2002) Activity theory and system design: A view from the trenches. *CSCW* 11, 55–80. DOI: 10.1023/A:1015219918601 Cited on page(s) 58, 59

Cooper, G. (1991) *Representing the User*. Unpublished Ph.D. Thesis, Open University, UK. Cited on page(s) 49, 84

Crabtree, A., Rodden, T., Tolmie, P. and Button, G. (2009) Ethnography considered harmful. *Proc. of CHI'09*, ACM, 879–888. DOI: 10.1145/1518701.1518835 Cited on page(s) 50

Craik, K.J.W. (1943) *The Nature of Explanation*. Cambridge University Press, Cambridge. Cited on page(s) 27

De Souza, C.S. (2005) *The Semiotic Engineering of Human–Computer Interaction*. MIT Press, Cambridge. Cited on page(s) 54

Dourish, P. (2001) *Where the Action Is: The Foundations of Embodied Interaction*. MIT Press, Cambridge. Cited on page(s) 14, 18, 76

Dourish, P. (2006) Implications for Design. *Proc. CHI'06*, ACM, 541–550. DOI: 10.1145/1124772.1124855 Cited on page(s) 50

Dourish, P. (2007) Responsibilities and implications: further thoughts on ethnography and design. *Proc. of DUX'07*, 25. DOI: 10.1145/1389908.1389941 Cited on page(s) 50, 51

Dourish, P., Finlay, J., Sengers, P. and Wright, P. (2004b) Reflective HCI: Towards a critical technical practice. In *CHI'04 Extended Abstracts*, ACM, 1727–1728. DOI: 10.1145/985921.986203 Cited on page(s) 65

Dourish, P., Grinter, R.E., Delgado de la Flor, J. and Joseph, M. (2004a) Security in the wild: User strategies for managing security as an everyday, practical problem. *Personal and Ubiquitous Computing* 8, 391–401. DOI: 10.1007/s00779-004-0308-5 Cited on page(s) 61

Draper, S. (1992) Book review: The new direction for HCI? "Through the Interface: A Human Activity Approach to User Interface Design," by S. Bødker, *International Journal of Man-Machine Studies* 37(6), 812–821. Cited on page(s) 31

Edge, D. and Blackwell, A. (2006) Correlates of the cognitive dimensions for tangible user interface. *Journal of Visual Languages and Computing (JVLC)* 17(4), 366–394. DOI: 10.1016/j.jvlc.2006.04.005 Cited on page(s) 36

Engestrøm, Y. (1990) *Learning, Working and Imagining: Twelve Studies in Activity Theory*. Orienta-Konsultit, Helsinki. Cited on page(s) 58

Erickson, T. (2002) Theory: A designer's view. *CSCW* 11, 269–270. Cited on page(s) 1, 81

Fallman, D. (2011) The new good: exploring the potential of philosophy of technology to contribute to human-computer interaction. *Proc. of CHI'11*, ACM, 1051–1060. DOI: 10.1145/1978942.1979099 Cited on page(s) 69

Flor, N.V. and Hutchins, E. (1992) Analyzing distributed cognition in software teams: a case study of collaborative programming during adaptive software maintenance. In Koenemann-Belliveau, J., Moher, T. and Robertson, T., Eds., *Empirical Studies of Programmers: Fourth Workshop*. Ablex, Norwood, NJ, 36–64. Cited on page(s) 39

Friedman, B., Smith, I.E., Kahn, P.H., Consolvo, S. and Selawski, J. (2006) Development of a privacy addendum for open source licenses: Value sensitive design in industry, *Proc. Ubicomp'06*, 194–211. DOI: 10.1007/11853565_12 Cited on page(s) 69

Furniss, D. and Blandford, A. (2006) Understanding emergency medical dispatch in terms of distributed cognition: A case study, *Ergonomics* 49(12,13), 1174–1203. DOI: 10.1080/00140130600612663 Cited on page(s) 39

Furniss, D. and Blandford, A. (2010) DiCoT modeling: From analysis to design. *Proc. CHI 2010, Workshop Bridging the Gap: Moving from Contextual Analysis to Design.* Cited on page(s) 40

Furniss, D., Blandford, A. and Curzon, P. (2011) Confessions from a grounded theory Ph.D.: Experiences and lessons learnt. In *Proc. CHI'11,* ACM, 113–122. DOI: 10.1145/1978942.1978960 Cited on page(s) 61, 62

Gabrielli, S., Rogers, Y. and Scaife, M. (2000) Young children's spatial representations developed through exploration of a desktop virtual reality scene. *Education and Information Technologies* 5(4), 251–262. DOI: 10.1023/A:1012097322806 Cited on page(s) 34

Garbis, C. and Waern, Y. (1999) Team co-ordination and communication in a rescue command staff – The role of public representations. *Le Travail Humain* 62(3), Special issue on Human-Machine Co-operation, 273–291. Cited on page(s) 39

Garfinkel, H. (1967) *Studies in Ethnomethodology.* Polity Press, Cambridge. Cited on page(s) 32, 48

Garfinkel, H. (2002) *Ethnomethodology's Program: Working out Durkheim's Aphorism.* Rowman and Littlefield, Lanham, MD. Cited on page(s) 48

Garfinkel, H. and Sacks, H. (1970) On the formal structures of practical action. In McKinney, J. and Tiryakian, E., Eds., *Theoretical Sociology.* Appleton-Century-Crifts, New York, 338–386. Cited on page(s) 32, 48

Garrett, J.J. (2010) The elements of user experience: User centered design for the Web and beyond. *Easy Riders.* Cited on page(s) xi

Gaver, B. (1991) Technology affordances. In *CHI'91 Conference Proc.* Addison-Wesley, Reading, MA, 85–90. DOI: 10.1145/108844.108856 Cited on page(s) 31, 42, 43

Gaver, B. (2008) A source of stimulation: Gibson's account of the environment. In Erickson, T. and McDonald, D.W., Eds., *HCI Remixed.* MIT, Cambridge, MA, 269–274. Cited on page(s) 42

Gaver, B., Beaver, J. and Benford, S. (2003) Ambiguity as a resource for design. *Proc. of CHI'03,* ACM, 233–240. DOI: 10.1145/642611.642653 Cited on page(s) 71, 82

Gaver, B., Bowers, J., Boucher, A., Gellersen, H., Pennington, S., Schmidt, A., Steed, A., Villar, N. and Walker, B. (2004) The drift table: Designing for ludic engagement. *Proc. CHI'04 Extended Abstracts,* 885–900. DOI: 10.1145/985921.985947 Cited on page(s) 71

Geertz, C. (1993) *The Interpretation of Cultures: Selected Essays.* Fontana Press, London. Cited on page(s) 48

Gerson, E.M. and Star, S.L. (1986) Analyzing due process in the workplace. *ACM Transactions on Office Information Systems* 4(3), 257–270. DOI: 10.1145/214427.214431 Cited on page(s) 52

Gibson, J.J. (1966) *The Senses Considered as Perceptual Systems.* Houghton-Mifflin, Boston. Cited on page(s) 42

Gibson, J.J. (1979) *The Ecological Approach to Visual Perception.* Houghton-Mifflin, Boston. Cited on page(s) 42

Gigerenzer, G., Todd, P.M., and the ABC Research Group (1999) *Simple Heuristics That Make Us Smart.* Oxford University Press, New York. Cited on page(s) 74

Glaser, B.G. (1992) *Basics of Grounded Theory: Emergence vs. Forcing*, Sociology Press, Mill Valley, CA. Cited on page(s) 60

Glaser, B.G. and Strauss, A. (1967) *Discovery of Grounded Theory.* Aldine, London. Cited on page(s) 60

González, V. (2006) *The Nature of Managing Multiple Activities in the Workplace.* Doctoral dissertation in Information and Computer Science, University of California, Irvine. Cited on page(s) 59

Green, T.R.G. (1989) Cognitive dimensions of notations. In Sutcliffe, A. and Macaulay, L., Eds., *People and Computers V.* Cambridge University Press, Cambridge, 443–459. Cited on page(s) 35

Green, T.R.G. (1990) The cognitive dimension of viscosity: a sticky problem for HCI. In Diaper, D., Gilmore, D., Cockton, G. and Shakel, B., Eds., *Human-Computer Interaction – INTERACT'90.* Elsevier Publishers, B.V., North Holland, Amsterdam, 79–86. Cited on page(s) 35

Green, T.R.G., Davies, S.P. and Gilmore, D.J. (1996) Delivering cognitive psychology to HCI: The problems of common language and of knowledge transfer. *Interacting with Computers* 8(1), 89–111. DOI: 10.1016/0953-5438(95)01020-3 Cited on page(s) 22, 31, 36

Greif, I. (1988) *Computer-Supported Cooperative Work: A Book of Readings.* Morgan Kaufmann, San Francisco, CA. Cited on page(s) 3

Grinter, R. (1998) Recomposition: Putting it all back together again. In *Proc. of CSCW'98*, ACM, 393–403. DOI: 10.1145/289444.289514 Cited on page(s) 61

Grinter, B. (2011) Grounded theory. Downloaded on 20/03/12 http://beki70.wordpress.com/ 2010/08/30/grounded-theory/ Cited on page(s) 62

Grudin, J. (1990) The computer reaches out: the historical continuity of interface design. *Proc. CHI'90,* ACM, 261–268. DOI: 10.1145/97243.97284 Cited on page(s) 7

Grudin, J. (2002) HCI theory is like the public library. Posting to CHIplace online discussion forum. Downloaded on Oct 15, 2002, www.chiplace.org Cited on page(s) 15

Grudin, J. (2006) Is HCI homeless?: In search of inter-disciplinary status. *Interactions* 13(1), 54–59. DOI: 10.1145/1151314.1151346 Cited on page(s) 11, 13

Grudin, J. (2007) Living without parental controls: The future of HCI. *Interactions* 14(2), 48–52. DOI: 10.1145/1229863.1229893 Cited on page(s) 11

Grudin, J. (2008) McGrath and the Behavior of Groups (BOGS). In Erickson, T. and McDonald, D.W., Eds., *HCI Remixed: Reflections on works that have influenced the HCI community*, 105–110, MIT Press, Cambridge, MA. Cited on page(s) 15, 52, 53

Grudin, J. (2012) Introduction: A moving target—The evolution of human–computer interaction. To appear in Jacko, J., Ed., *Human-Computer Interaction Handbook: Fundamentals, evolving technologies, and emerging applications*, 3rd ed., Taylor and Francis. DOI: 10.1201/b11963 Cited on page(s) xi, 1, 12, 65

Gunther, V.A., Burns, D.J. and Payne, D.J. (1986) Text editing performance as a function of training with command terms of differing lengths and frequencies. *SIGCHI Bulletin* 18, 57–59. DOI: 10.1145/15683.1044091 Cited on page(s) 23

Hall, E.T. (1963) A system for the notation of proxemic research. *American Anthropologist* 65, 1003–1026. DOI: 10.1525/aa.1963.65.5.02a00020 Cited on page(s) 79

Hallnäs, L. and Redström, J. (2002) From use to presence: On the expressions and aesthetics of every-day computational things. *ACM Transactions on Computer-Human Interaction* 9(2), 106–124. DOI: 10.1145/513665.513668 Cited on page(s) 68

Halloran, J., Rogers, Y. and Scaife, M. (2002) Taking the 'no' out of lotus notes: Activity theory, groupware and student work projects. In *Proc. of CSCL*. Lawrence Erlbaum Associates, Inc., Hillsdale, NJ, 169–178. DOI: 10.3115/1658616.1658641 Cited on page(s) 58

Halverson, C.A. (1995) *Inside the Cognitive Workplace: New Technology and Air Traffic Control*. Ph.D. Thesis, Dept. of Cognitive Science, University of California, San Diego, CA. Cited on page(s) 39

Halverson, C.A. (2002) Activity theory and distributed cognition: Or what does CSCW need to DO with theories? *CSCW* 11, 243–275. DOI: 10.1023/A:1015298005381 Cited on page(s) 17, 40, 58, 89

Harper, R., Rodden, T., Rogers, Y. and Sellen, A. (2008) *Being Human: HCI in the Year 2020*. Microsoft. Cited on page(s) 3, 12, 65, 66, 67

Harrison, S., Sengers, P. and Tatar, D. (2011) Making epistemological trouble: Third-paradigm HCI as successor science. *Interacting with Computers* 23(5), 385–392. DOI: 10.1016/j.intcom.2011.03.005 Cited on page(s) xii, 12, 78

Harrison, S., Tatar, D. and Sengers, P. (2007) The three paradigms of HCI. *CHI 2007*. San Jose, CA. DOI: 10.1234/12345678 Cited on page(s) xii, 7, 12, 13, 65, 78

Hassenzahl, M. (2001) The effect of perceived hedonic quality on product appealingness. *International Journal of Human-Computer Interaction* 13(4), 481–499. DOI: 10.1207/S15327590IJHC1304_07 Cited on page(s) 12

Hayes, G. (2011) The relationship of action research to human-computer interaction. *ACM Transactions on Computer-Human Interaction* 18(3), article 15, 20 pages. DOI: 10.1145/1993060.1993065 Cited on page(s) 66

Heath, C. and Luff, P. (1991) Collaborative activity and technological design: Task coordination in London underground control rooms. In *Proc. of the Second European Conference on Computer-Supported Cooperative Work*. Kluwer, Dordrecht, 65–80. DOI: 10.1007/978-94-011-3506-1_5 Cited on page(s) 32, 48

Heidegger, M. (1996). Being and Time. 1927. Trans. Joan Stambaugh, Albany: SUNY. Cited on page(s) 76

Hollan, J., Hutchins, E. and Kirsh, D. (2000) Distributed cognition: Toward a new foundation for human-computer interaction research. *Transactions on Human-Computer Interaction* 7(2), 174–196. DOI: 10.1145/353485.353487 Cited on page(s) 13, 41

Holtzblatt, K. and Jones, S. (1993) Contextual inquiry: A participatory technique for systems design. In Schuler, D. and Namioka, A., Eds., *Participatory Design: Principles and Practice*. Lawrence Erlbaum Associates, Hillsdale, NJ, 177–210. Cited on page(s) 40

Hornecker, E. and Buur, J. (2006). Getting a grip on tangible interaction: A framework on physical space and social interaction. *Proc. CHI'06*, ACM, 437–446. DOI: 10.1145/1124772.1124838 Cited on page(s) 77

Hornecker, E. and Nicol, E. (2012) What do lab-based user studies tell us about in-the-wild behavior? Insights from a study of museum interactives. To appear in *Proc. DIS'12*, ACM. Cited on page(s) 73

Hornecker, E., Marshall, P. and Rogers, Y. (2007) Entry and access – how shareability comes about. *Proc. of DPPI'07*, (Designing Pleasurable Products and Interfaces). ACM, Helsinki, 328–342. Cited on page(s) 44

Hughes, J.A., O'Brien, J., Rodden, T., Rouncefield, M. and Blythin, S. (1997) Designing with ethnography: a presentation framework for design. *Proc. DIS'97*, ACM, 147–158. DOI: 10.1145/263552.263598 Cited on page(s) 47

Hurtienne, J. (2009) Cognition in HCI: An ongoing story. *Human Technology*, 5(1), 12–28. Cited on page(s) 12, 14, 78

Hutchins, E. (1995) *Cognition in the Wild.* MIT Press, Cambridge, MA. Cited on page(s) 31, 37, 38, 73

Hutchins, E., Hollan, J.D. and Norman, D. (1986) Direct manipulation interfaces. In Draper, S. and Norman, D., Eds., *User Centred System Design.* Lawrence Erlbaum Associates, Hillsdale, NJ, 87–124. Cited on page(s) 23, 24

Hutchins, E. and Klausen, T. (1996) Distributed cognition in an airline cockpit. In Middleton, D. and Engeström, Y., Eds., *Communication and Cognition at Work.* Cambridge University Press, Cambridge, MA, 15–34. Cited on page(s) 39

Hutchins, E. and Palen, L. (1997) Constructing meaning from space, gesture and speech. In Resnick, L.B., Saljo, R., Pontecorvo, C. and Burge, B., Eds., *Discourse, Tools, and Reasoning: Essays on Situated Cognition.* Springer-Verlag, Heidelberg, Germany, 23–40. Cited on page(s) 39

Ihde, D. (1993) *Philosophy of Technology: An Introduction.* Paragon House, Salt Lake City, UT. Cited on page(s) 69

Jacob, R. (1996) Human-computer interaction: Input devices. *ACM Computer Survey* 28(1), 177–179. DOI: 10.1145/234313.234387 Cited on page(s) 5

John, B.E. and Gray, W.D. (1995) CPM-GOMS: An analysis method for tasks with parallel activities. In *Conference companion on Human factors in computing systems (CHI'95)*, ACM, 393–394. DOI: 10.1145/223355.223738 Cited on page(s) 26

Johnson, M. (1987) *The Body in the Mind: The Bodily Basis of Meaning, Imagination, and Reason.* University of Chicago, Chicago, IL. Cited on page(s) 78

Johnson, J. and Henderson, A. (2012) *Conceptual Models: Core to Good Design.* Morgan & Claypool Publishers, San Rafael, CA. DOI: 10.2200/S00391ED1V01Y201111HCI012 Cited on page(s) 78

Johnson-Laird, P.N. (1983) *Mental Models.* Cambridge University Press, Cambridge. Cited on page(s) 27

Kadoda, G., Stone, R. and Diaper, D. (1999) Desirable features of educational theorem provers - A cognitive dimensions viewpoint. In Green, T.R.G., Abdullah, R. and Brna, P., Eds., *Collected Papers of the 11th Annual Workshop of the Psychology of Programming Interest Group (PPIG- 11)*, 18–23. Cited on page(s) 36

Kaptelinin, V. (1996) Computer-mediated activity: Functional organs in social and developmental contexts. In Nardi, B., Ed., *Context and Consciousness: Activity Theory and Human-Computer Interaction.* MIT Press, Cambridge, MA, 45–68. Cited on page(s) 13

Kaptelinin, V. and Nardi, B.A. (1997) Activity theory: Basic concepts and applications. *Tutorial Notes, Proc. CHI'97*, ACM. DOI: 10.1007/3-540-60614-9_14 Cited on page(s) 55

Kaptelinin, V., Nardi, B.A. and Macaulay, C. (1999) The activity checklist: A tool for representing the "space" of context. *Interactions*, 27–39. DOI: 10.1145/306412.306431 Cited on page(s) 55

Karat, J. (Ed.) (1991) *Taking Software Design Seriously: Practical Techniques for Human–Computer Interaction Design*. Academic Press, San Diego. Cited on page(s) 68

Karau, S.J. and Williams, K.D. (1993) Social loafing: A meta-analytic review and theoretical integration. *Journal of Personality and Social Psychology* 65(4), 681–706. DOI: 10.1037/0022-3514.65.4.681 Cited on page(s) 53

Kendon. A. (1990) *Conducting Interaction: Patterns of Behavior in Focused Encounters*. Cambridge University Press, Cambridge. Cited on page(s) 79

Kieras, D. and Meyer, D.E. (1997) An overview of the EPIC architecture for cognition and performance with application to human-computer interaction. *Human–Computer Interaction* 12, 391–438. DOI: 10.1207/s15327051hci1204_4 Cited on page(s) 26

Kirsh, D. (1997) Interactivity and multimedia interfaces. *Instructional Science* 25, 79–96. DOI: 10.1023/A:1002915430871 Cited on page(s) 28, 31, 33

Kirsh, D. (2001) The context of work. *HCI* 6(2), 306–322. DOI: 10.1207/S15327051HCI16234_12 Cited on page(s) 42, 44

Kirsh, D. (2010) Thinking with external representations. *AI and Society*. Springer, London, 25, 441–454. DOI: 10.1007/s00146-010-0272-8 Cited on page(s) 33

Klemmer, S.R. Hartmann, B. and Takayama, L. (2006) How bodies matter: Five themes for interaction design. *Proc. of DIS'06*, ACM, 140–149. DOI: 10.1145/1142405.1142429 Cited on page(s) 77

Kraut, R.E. (2003) Applying social psychological theory to the problems of group work. In Carroll, J., Ed., *HCI Models, Theories, and Frameworks: Toward a Multidisciplinary Science*. Morgan-Kaufmann Publishers, New York, 325–356. Cited on page(s) 14, 53

Kuhn, T.S. (1962) *The Structure of Scientific Revolutions*. University of Chicago Press, Chicago. Cited on page(s) 13

Kuutti, K. (1996) Activity theory as a potential framework for human-computer interaction research. In Nardi, B., Ed., *Context and Consciousness: Activity Theory and Human-Computer Interaction*. MIT Press, Cambridge, MA, 17–44. Cited on page(s) 55, 56

Landauer, T.K. (1991) Let's get real: A position paper on the role of cognitive psychology in the design of humanly useful and usable systems. In Carroll, J., Ed., *Designing Interaction: Psychology at the Human-Computer Interface*. Cambridge University Press, New York, 60–73. Cited on page(s) 13, 22, 81

Larkin, J.H. and Simon, H.A. (1987) Why a diagram is (sometimes) worth ten thousand words. *Cognitive Science* 11, 65–99. DOI: 10.1111/j.1551-6708.1987.tb00863.x Cited on page(s) 32

Latour, B. (2005) *Reassembling the Social: An Introduction to Actor-Network-Theory*. Oxford University Press, Oxford. Cited on page(s) 54

Law, J. (1987) Technology and heterogeneous engineering: The case of portuguese expansion. In Bijker, W.E., Hughes, T.P. and Pinch, T.J., Eds., *The Social Construction of Technological Systems: New Directions in the Sociology and History of Technology*. MIT Press, Cambridge, MA. Cited on page(s) 54

Ledgard, H., Singer, A. and Whiteside, J. (1981) Directions in human factors for interactive systems. In Goos, G. and Hartmanis, J., Eds., *Lecture Notes in Computer Science* 103, Springer-Verlag, Berlin. Cited on page(s) 23

Leontiev, A.N. (1978) *Activity, Consciousness and Personality*. Prentice Hall, Englewood Cliffs, NJ. Cited on page(s) 55

Leontiev, A.N. (1981) *Problems of the Development of Mind*. Progress, Moscow. Cited on page(s) 57

Leontiev, A.N. (1989) The problem of activity in the history of Soviet psychology. *Soviet Psychology* 27(1), 22–39. DOI: 10.2753/RPO1061-0405270122 Cited on page(s) 55

Lewin, K. (1951) *Field Theory in Social Science: Selected Theoretical Papers*. (Edited by Dorwin Cartwright.) Oxford University Press, Oxford. Cited on page(s) 9

Lidwell, W., Holden, K. and Butler, J. (2006) *Universal Principles of Design*. Rockport Publishers, Inc., Minneapolis, MN. Cited on page(s) 44

Light, A. (2009) Democratising technology: A method, in designing for the 21st century. In Inns, T., Ed., *Interdisciplinary Methods and Findings*. Ashgate Publishing, Surrey, UK. Cited on page(s) 69

Long, J. (1991) Theory in human-computer interaction? *IEE Colloquium on Theory in Human-Computer Interaction* 2, 1–6. Cited on page(s) 13, 81

Long, J. and Dowell, J. (1989) Conceptions for the discipline of HCI: Craft, applied science, and engineering. In Sutcliffe, A. and Macaulay, L., Eds., *People and Computers V*, Cambridge University Press, Cambridge, UK, 9–32. Cited on page(s) 31

Long, J. and Dowell, J. (1996) Cognitive engineering human-computer interactions. In *The Psychologist*, July, 313–317. Cited on page(s) 31

Löwgren. J. and Stolterman, E. (2004) *Thoughtful Interaction Design*. MIT Press, Cambridge, MA. Cited on page(s) xii, 68

MacKay, W.E., Ratzer, A.V. and Janecek, P. (2000) Video artefacts for design: Bridging the gap between abstraction and detail. In *Proc. of DIS 2000*, 72–82. DOI: 10.1145/347642.347666 Cited on page(s) 56

Maglio, P., Matlock, T., Raphaely, D., Chernicky, B. and Kirsh D. (1999) Interactive skill in scrabble. In *Proc. of the Twenty-first Annual Conference of the Cognitive Science Society*. Lawrence Erlbaum, Mahwah, NJ. Cited on page(s) 33

Malone, T.W. and Crowston, K. (1990) What is coordination theory and how can it help design cooperative work systems. *Proc. of CSCW'90*, ACM, 357–370. DOI: 10.1145/99332.99367 Cited on page(s) 54

Mancini, C. (2011) Animal-computer interaction (ACI): a manifesto. *Interactions* 18(4), 69–73. DOI: 10.1145/1978822.1978836 Cited on page(s) 67

Mantovani, G. (1996) Social context in HCI: A new framework for mental models, cooperation and communication. *Cognitive Science* 20, 237–269. DOI: 10.1207/s15516709cog2002_3 Cited on page(s) 63

Marshall, P., Hornecker, E. and Rogers, Y. (2013) Embodiment in HCI. Submitted to *TOCHI*. Cited on page(s) 76

Marshall, P., Morris, R., Rogers, Y., Kreitmayer, S. and Davies, M. (2011a) Rethinking 'multi-user': An in-the-wild study of how groups approach a walk-up-and-use tabletop interface. *Proc. of CHI'11*, ACM, 3033–3042. DOI: 10.1145/1978942.1979392 Cited on page(s) 73

Marshall, P., Rogers, Y. and Pantidi, N. (2011b) Using F-formations to analyse spatial patterns of interaction in physical environments. *Proc. of CSCW'11*, ACM, 445–454. DOI: 10.1145/1958824.1958893 Cited on page(s) 79

Masterman, E. and Rogers, Y. (2002) A framework for designing interactive multimedia to scaffold young children's understanding of historical chronology. *Instructional Science* 30, 221–241. DOI: 10.1023/A:1015133106888 Cited on page(s) 34

McCarthy, J. and Wright, P. (2004) *Technology as Experience*. MIT Press, Cambridge, MA. Cited on page(s) 69

McGrath, J. (1984) *Groups, Interactions, and Performance*. Prentice Hall, Englewood Cliffs, NJ. Cited on page(s) 52

McGrath, J.E. (1991) Time, interaction, and performance (TIP): A theory of groups. *Small Group Research* 22(2), 147–174. DOI: 10.1177/1046496491222001 Cited on page(s) 52

McKnight, J. and Doherty, G. (2008) Distributed cognition and mobile healthcare work, in people and computers XXII: culture creativity interaction. *Proc. of HCI 2008,* The 22nd British HCI Group Annual Conference. Cited on page(s) 41

Modugno, F.M., Green, T.R.G. and Myers, B. (1994) Visual programming in a visual domain: A case study of cognitive dimensions. In Cockton, G., Draper, S.W. and Weir, G.R.S., Eds., *People and Computers IX.* Cambridge University Press, Cambridge, UK. Cited on page(s) 36

Mohlich, R. and Nielsen, J. (1990) Improving a human-computer dialogue. *Comm. of the ACM* 33(3), 338–48. DOI: 10.1145/77481.77486 Cited on page(s) 26

Monk, A. (Ed.) (1984) *Fundamentals of Human-Computer Interaction.* Academic Press, London. Cited on page(s) 21

Mumford, E. and Weir, M. (1979) *Computer Systems in Work Design-The ETHICS method.* Wiley, New York. Cited on page(s) 52

Nardi, B.A. (Ed.) (1996) *Context and Consciousness: Activity Theory and Human-Computer Interaction.* MIT Press, Cambridge, MA. Cited on page(s) 40, 47, 55, 56, 85

Nardi, B.A. (2002) Coda and response to Christine Halverson. *CSCW,* 269–275. DOI: 10.1023/A:1015293915392 Cited on page(s) 40

Nardi, B.A. and Johnson, J. (1994) User preferences for task-specific versus generic application software. In *CHI'94 Proc.,* ACM, New York, 392–398. DOI: 10.1145/191666.191796 Cited on page(s) 56

Nardi, B.A. and Kaptelinin, V. (2012) *Activity Theory in HCI: Fundamentals and Reflections.* Morgan & Claypool Publishers, San Rafael, CA. DOI: 10.2200/S00413ED1V01Y201203HCI013 Cited on page(s) 55

Neisser, U. (1985) Toward an ecologically oriented cognitive science. In Schlecter, T.M. and Toglia, M.P., Eds., *New Directions in Cognitive Science.* Ablex Publishing Corp, Norwood, NJ, 17–32. Cited on page(s) 42

Norman, D. (1983) Some observations on mental models. In Gentner, D. and Stevens, A.L., Eds., *Mental Models.* Lawrence Erlbaum Associates, Hillsdale, NJ. Cited on page(s) 28

Norman, D. (1986) Cognitive engineering. In Draper, S. and Norman, D., Eds., *User Centered System Design.* Lawrence Erlbaum Associates, Hillsdale, NJ, 31–61. Cited on page(s) 23

Norman, D. (1988) *The Psychology of Everyday Things.* Basic Books, New York. Cited on page(s) 21, 31, 42, 43

Norman, D. (1993) Cognition in the head and in the world. *Cognitive Science* 17(1), 1–6. Cited on page(s) 33

Norman, D. (1999) Affordances, conventions and design. *Interactions,* May/June 1999, 38–42, ACM, New York. Cited on page(s) 43

Oliver, M. (1997) *Visualisation and Manipulation Tools for Modal Logic,* Unpublished Ph.D. thesis, Open University, Milton Keynes, UK. Cited on page(s) 36

Olson, J.S. and Olson, G.M. (1991) The growth of cognitive modelling since GOMS. *Human Computer Interaction* 5, 221–266. DOI: 10.1207/s15327051hci0502&3_4 Cited on page(s) 25, 26

O'Malley, C. and Draper, S. (1992) Representation and interaction: Are mental models all in the Mind? In Rogers, Y., Rutherford, A. and Bibby, P., Eds., *Models in the Mind: Theory, Perspective and Application.* Academic Press, London. Cited on page(s) 33

Otero, N. (2003) Interactivity in graphical representations: Assessing its benefits for learning. *Unpublished Dphil,* University of Sussex, Sussex, UK. Cited on page(s) 34

Patel, V.L. and Groen, G.J. (1993) Comparing apples and oranges: some dangers in confusing frameworks and theories. *Cognitive Science* 17, 135–141. DOI: 10.1207/s15516709cog1701_9 Cited on page(s) 85

Pirolli, P. and Card, S. (1997) The evolutionary ecology of information foraging. *Technical report, UIR-R97–01,* Palo Alto Research Center, Palo Alto, CA. Cited on page(s) 62

Plowman, L., Rogers, Y. and Ramage, M. (1995) What are workplace studies for? In *Proc. of the Fourth European Conference on Computer-Supported Cooperative Work.* Dordrecht, Kluwer, The Netherlands, 309–324. DOI: 10.1007/978-94-011-0349-7_20 Cited on page(s) 18, 47, 83, 84

Polson, P.G., Lewis, C., Rieman, J. and Wharton, C. (1992) Cognitive walkthroughs: a method for theory-based evaluation of user interfaces. *International Journal of Man-Machine Studies* 36, 741–73. DOI: 10.1016/0020-7373(92)90039-N Cited on page(s) 27

Preece, J., Rogers, Y., Sharp, H., Benyon, D. Holland, S. and Carey, T. (1994) *Human-Computer Interaction.* Addison-Wesley, London. Cited on page(s) 21

Preece, J., Sharp, H. and Rogers, Y. (2003) *Interaction Design: Beyond Human Computer-Interaction,* 1st ed., Wiley. Cited on page(s) xii, 3

Price, S. (2002) Diagram representation: the cognitive basis for understanding animation in education. *Unpublished Dphil,* University of Sussex, Sussex, UK. Cited on page(s) 34, 36

Price, S. and Rogers, Y. (2004) Let's get physical: the learning benefits of interacting in digitally augmented physical spaces. *Journal of Computers and Education* 43, 137–151. DOI: 10.1016/j.compedu.2003.12.009 Cited on page(s) 71

Rasmussen, J. and Rouse, W. (Eds.) (1981) *Human Detection and Diagnosis of System Failures.* Plenum Press, New York. Cited on page(s) 42

Robertson, T, (1997) Cooperative work and lived cognition: a taxonomy of embodied actions. *Proc. of ECSCW'07*, Kluwer Academic Publishers, 205–220. Cited on page(s) 76

Rodden, T., Rogers, Y., Halloran, J. and Taylor, I. (2003) Designing novel interactional work spaces to support face to face consultations. To appear in *CHI Proc.*, ACM. DOI: 10.1145/642611.642623 Cited on page(s) 35

Rogers, Y. (1993) Coordinating computer mediated work. *CSCW* 1, 295–315. DOI: 10.1007/BF00754332 Cited on page(s) 39

Rogers, Y. (1994) Exploring obstacles: Integrating CSCW in evolving organisations. In *CSCW'94 Proc.*, ACM, New York, 67–78. DOI: 10.1145/192844.192875 Cited on page(s) 39

Rogers, Y. (1997) Reconfiguring the Social Scientist: Shifting from telling designers what to do to getting more involved. In Bowker, G.C., Star, S.L., Turner, W. and Gasser, L., Eds., *Social Science, Technical Systems and Cooperative Work*, LEA, 57–77. Cited on page(s) 49, 50

Rogers, Y. (2004) New Theoretical approaches for human-computer interaction. *Annual Review of Information, Science and Technology* 38, 87–143. DOI: 10.1002/aris.1440380103 Cited on page(s) 5, 6, 17, 21

Rogers, Y. (2008a) When the external entered HCI: Designing effective representations. In Erickson, T. and McDonald, D., Eds., *HCI Remixed.* MIT Press, Cambridge, MA, 275–280. Cited on page(s) 33

Rogers, Y. (2008b) 57 varieties of activity theory. *Interacting with Computers* 20(2), 247–250. DOI: 10.1016/j.intcom.2007.07.004 Cited on page(s) 59

Rogers, Y. (2009) The changing face of human-computer interaction in the age of ubiquitous computing. *Proc. of USAB'09*, 1–19. DOI: 10.1007/978-3-642-10308-7_1 Cited on page(s) 11, 86

Rogers, Y. (2011) Interaction design gone wild: Striving for wild theory. *Interactions* 18(4), 58–62. DOI: 10.1145/1978822.1978834 Cited on page(s) 3, 14, 73, 74, 86

Rogers, Y., Connelly, K., Tedesco, L., Hazlewood, W., Kurtz, A., Hall, B., Hursey, J. and Toscos, T. (2007) Why it's worth the hassle: The value of in-situ studies when designing UbiComp. *UbiComp 2007*, LNCS 4717, Springer-Verlag, Berlin Heidelberg, 336–353. DOI: 10.1007/978-3-540-74853-3_20 Cited on page(s) 73

Rogers, Y., Lim, Y., Hazlewood, W., and Marshall, P. (2009) Equal opportunities: Do shareable interfaces promote more group participation than single users displays? *Human–Computer Interaction* 24(2), 79–116. DOI: 10.1080/07370020902739379 Cited on page(s) 44

Rogers, Y. and Muller, H. (2006) A framework for designing sensor-based interactions to promote exploration and reflection. *International Journal of Human Computer Studies* 64(1), 1–15. DOI: 10.1016/j.ijhcs.2005.05.004 Cited on page(s) 82

Rogers, Y., Preece, J. and Sharp, H. (2011) *Interaction Design: Beyond Human-Computer Interaction*, 3rd ed., Wiley, New York. Cited on page(s) xi, 2, 3, 4, 24

Rogers, Y., Price, S., Randell, C., Stanton-Fraser, D., Weal, M. and Fitzpatrick. G. (2005) Ubi-learning: Integrating outdoor and indoor learning experiences. *Comm. of ACM* 48(1), 55–59. DOI: 10.1145/1039539.1039570 Cited on page(s) 71

Rogers, Y., Rutherford, A. and Bibby, P. (Eds.) (1992) *Models in the Mind: Theory, Perspective and Application*. Academic Press, London. Cited on page(s) 27

Rogers, Y. and Scaife, M. (1998) How can interactive multimedia facilitate learning? In Lee, J., Ed., *Intelligence and Multimodality in Multimedia Interfaces: Research and Applications*. AAAI Press, Menlo Park, CA. Cited on page(s) 34

Sarker, S., Lau, F. and Sahay, S. (2001) Using an adapted grounded theory approach for inductive theory building about virtual team development. *The Data Base for Advances in Information Systems* 32(1), 38–56. DOI: 10.1145/506740.506745 Cited on page(s) 61

Satchell, C. (2008) Cultural theory and real word design: Dystopian and utopian outcomes. *Proc. of CHI'08*, ACM, 1593–1602. DOI: 10.1145/1357054.1357303 Cited on page(s) 71

Scaife, M. and Rogers, Y. (1996) External Cognition: How do graphical representations work? *International Journal of Human-Computer Studies* 45, 185–213. DOI: 10.1006/ijhc.1996.0048 Cited on page(s) 31, 34

Scaife, M., Halloran, J., and Rogers, Y.(2002) Let's work together: Supporting two-party collaborations with new forms of shared interactive representations. *Proc. of COOP'2002*. Nice, France, August 2002, IOS Press, The Netherlands, 123–138. Cited on page(s) 35

Scapin, D.L. (1981) Computer commands in restricted natural language: Some aspects of memory of experience. *Human Factors* 23, 365–375. DOI: 10.1177/001872088102300311 Cited on page(s) 23

Schmidt, K. (2011) *Cooperative Work and Coordinative Practices: Contributions to the Conceptual Foundations of Computer-Supported Cooperative Work (CSCW)*, Springer Verlag. Cited on page(s) 54

Scruton, R. (2012) Brain drain. *The Spectator*, 18–19. Cited on page(s) 71

Searle, J. (1969) *Speech Acts: An essay in the Philosophy of Language*. Cambridge University, Cambridge, England, UK. Cited on page(s) 53

Sengers, P. and Gaver, B. (2006) Staying open to interpretation: Engaging multiple meanings in design and evaluation. *Proc. DIS'06*, 99–108. DOI: 10.1145/1142405.1142422 Cited on page(s) 71

Shapiro, D. (1994) The limits of ethnography: Combining social sciences for CSCW. In *Proc. of CSCW'94*, ACM, New York, 417–428. DOI: 10.1145/192844.193064 Cited on page(s) 45

Sharp, H. and Robinson, H. (2008) Collaboration and co-ordination in mature eXtreme programming teams. *International Journal of Human-Computer Studies* 66, 506–518. DOI: 10.1016/j.ijhcs.2007.10.004 Cited on page(s) 41

Sharp, H., Rogers, Y. and Preece, J. (2007) *Interaction Design: Beyond Human-Computer Interaction*, 2nd ed., John Wiley, New York. Cited on page(s) 3

Shneiderman, B. (1983) Direct manipulation: A step beyond programming languages. *IEEE Computer* 16(8), 57–69. DOI: 10.1109/MC.1983.1654471 Cited on page(s) 23

Shneiderman, B. (2002a) *Leonardo's Laptop*. MIT Press, Cambridge, MA. Cited on page(s)

Shneiderman, B. (2011) Claiming success, charting the future: Micro-HCI and macro-HCI. *Interactions* 18(5), 10–11. DOI: 10.1145/2008176.2008180 Cited on page(s) xi, 1, 66

Shneiderman, B. (2012) Forward: The expanding impact of human-computer interaction. To appear in Jacko, J., Ed., *Handbook of Human-Computer Interaction*. Cited on page(s) 8

Shön, D. (1987) *Educating the Reflective Practitioner*. Jossey-Bass, San Francisco, CA. Cited on page(s) 68

SIGCHI (2012) Bylaws. Downloaded 28/03/12, http://www.sigchi.org/about/bylaws#a1 Cited on page(s) 2

Spasser, M. (2002) Realist activity theory for digital library evaluation: Conceptual framework and case study. *CSCW* 11, 81–110. DOI: 10.1023/A:1015288305397 Cited on page(s) 58

St. Amant, R. (1999) User interface affordance in a planning representation. *Human-Computer Interaction* 14, 317–354. DOI: 10.1207/S15327051HCI1403_3 Cited on page(s) 43

Star, S.L. (1996) Working together: Symbolic interactionism, activity theory and information systems. In Engeström, Y. and Middleton, D., Eds., *Cognition and Communication at Work*. Cambridge University Press, Cambridge, UK, 296–318. Cited on page(s) 62

Stiles, K. (1996) Art and Technology. In Stiles, K. and Seltz, P., Eds., *Theories and Documents of Contemporary Art.* University of California Press, Berkely, CA. Cited on page(s) 65

Strauss, A. and Corbin, J. (1998) *Basics of Qualitative Research: Techniques and Procedures for Developing Grounded Theory,* 2nd ed., Sage, London. Cited on page(s) 60, 61

Stringer, E.T. (2007) *Action Research.* Sage, London. Cited on page(s) 66

Suchman, L.A. (1983) Office procedure as practical action: Models of work and system design. *TOIS* 1(4), 320–328. DOI: 10.1145/357442.357445 Cited on page(s) 46

Suchman, L.A. (1987) *Plans and Situated Actions.* Cambridge University Press, Cambridge, UK. Cited on page(s) 18, 45, 46, 76

Sutcliffe, A. (2000) On the effective use and reuse of HCI knowledge. *Transactions on Computer-Human Interaction* 7(2), 197–221. DOI: 10.1145/353485.353488 Cited on page(s) 13, 26, 34, 35

Taylor, A.S. (2011) Out there. *Proc. of CHI'11,* ACM, 685–694. Cited on page(s) 13, 67

Teo, L. and John, B.E. (2008) CogTool-explorer: Towards a tool for predicting user interaction. *Proc. of CHI EA'08,* ACM, 2793–2798. DOI: 10.1145/1358628.1358763 Cited on page(s) 26

Todd, P., Rogers, Y. and Payne, S. (2011) Nudging the trolley in the supermarket: How to deliver the right information to shoppers. *International Journal on Mobile HCI (IJMHCI)* 3(2), 20–34. Cited on page(s) 14, 75

Vanderheiden, G.C. (2008) Ubiquitous accessibility, common technology core, and micro assistive technology. *ACM Transactions in Accessible Computing* 1(2), 10.1–7. DOI: 10.1145/1408760.1408764 Cited on page(s) 69

Vicente, K.J. (1995) A few implications of an ecological approach to human factors. In Flach, J., Hancock, P., Carid, J. and Vicente, K.J., Eds., *Global Perspective on the Ecology of Human-Machine Systems,* 54–67. Cited on page(s) 42, 43

Vicente, K.J. and Rasmussen, J. (1990) The ecology of man-machine systems II: Mediating 'direct perception' in complex work domains. *Ecological Psychology* 2, 207–249. DOI: 10.1207/s15326969eco0203_2 Cited on page(s) 44

von Neumann, J. and Morgenstern, O. (1944) *Theory of Games and Economic Behavior.* Princeton University Press, Princeton, NJ. Cited on page(s) 74

Vygotsky, L.S. (1962) *Thought and Language.* MIT Press, Cambridge, MA. DOI: 10.1037/11193-000 Cited on page(s) 55

Weiser, M. (1991) The computer for the 21st Century. *Scientific American* 265(3), 94–104. DOI: 10.1038/scientificamerican0991-94 Cited on page(s) 5, 12

Winograd, T. (1994) Categories, disciplines, and social coordination. *Journal of Computer-Supported Cooperative Work* 2, 191–197. DOI: 10.1007/BF00749016 Cited on page(s) 54

Winograd, T. (Ed.) (1996) *Bringing Design to Software*. Addison-Wesley, Reading, MA. Cited on page(s) 68

Winograd, T. (1997) From computing machinery to interaction design. In Denning, P. and Metcalfe, R., Eds., *Beyond Calculation: The Next Fifty Years of Computing*. Springer-Verlag, 149–162. Cited on page(s) 68

Winograd, T. and Flores, F. (1986) *Understanding Computers and Cognition: A New Foundation for Design*. Intellect Books, Bristol, UK. Cited on page(s) 53, 76

Woods, D.D. (1995) Toward a theoretical base for representation design in the computer medium: ecological perception and aiding cognition. In Flach, J., Hancock, P., Carid, J. and Vicente, K.J., Eds., *Global Perspective on the Ecology of Human-Machine Systems*, 157–188. Cited on page(s) 36, 42

Wright, P. and McCarthy, J. (2010) *Experience-Centered Design*. Morgan & Claypool's Publishers, San Rafael, CA. DOI: 10.2200/S00229ED1V01Y201003HCI009 Cited on page(s) 70

Wright, P., Fields, R. and Harrison, M. (2000) Analysing human-computer interaction as distributed cognition: The resources model. *Human Computer Interaction* 51(1), 1–41. DOI: 10.1207/S15327051HCI1501_01 Cited on page(s) 31, 33, 35, 36

Yamazaki, K., Yamazaki, A., Okada, M., Kuno, Y., Kobayashi, Y., Hoshi, Y., Pitsch, K., Luff, P., vom Lehn, D. and Heath, C. (2009) Revealing Gauguin: engaging visitors in robot guide's explanation in an art museum. *Proc. of CHI'09*, ACM, 1437–1446. DOI: 10.1145/1518701.1518919 Cited on page(s) 49

Yang, S., Burnett, M.M., Dekoven, E. and Zloof, M. (1995) Representations design benchmarks: A design-time aid for VPL navigable static representations. *Dept. of Computer Science Technical Report 95–60-4*. Oregon State University, Corvallis, OR. DOI: 10.1006/jvlc.1997.0047 Cited on page(s) 36

Yuill, N. and Rogers, Y. (2012) Mechanisms for collaboration: A design and evaluation framework for multi-user interfaces. *TOCHI*. DOI: 10.1145/2147783.2147784 Cited on page(s) 83

Author's Biography

YVONNE ROGERS

Yvonne Rogers is the director of the Interaction Centre at UCL and a professor of Interaction Design. She is internationally renowned for her work in HCI and ubiquitous computing. She is also a visiting professor at the Open University, Indiana University, and Sussex University and has spent sabbaticals at Stanford, Apple, Queensland University, UCSD, and University of Cape Town. Her research focuses on augmenting and extending everyday learning and work activities with a diversity of novel technologies. She was one of the principal investigators on the UK Equator Project (2000–2007) where she pioneered ubiquitous learning. She has published widely, beginning with her Ph.D. work on graphical interfaces to her recent work on public visualizations and behavioral change. She has also been awarded a prestigious *EPSRC dream fellowship* where she is rethinking the relationship between aging, computing, and creativity.

Central to her work is a critical stance towards how visions, theories, and frameworks can shape the fields of HCI, cognitive science, and Ubicomp. She has been instrumental in promulgating new theories (e.g., external cognition), alternative methodologies (e.g., in-the-wild studies), and far-reaching research agendas (e.g., *Being Human: HCI in 2020* manifesto). She is also a co-author of the definitive textbook on Interaction Design and HCI now in its 3rd edition that has sold over 150,000 copies worldwide. She is a Fellow of the British Computer Society and the ACM's CHI Academy.

CPSIA information can be obtained
at www.ICGtesting.com
Printed in the USA
LVOW05s1447021017
550895LV00010B/171/P